A GIRLFRIENDS'
Getaway

GFG

A Woman's Guide to
Traveling With Your Girls

Vikki Miller-Walton

Print ISBN: 978-1-54396-092-1
eBook ISBN: 978-1-54396-093-8

Dedication And Acknowledgements

With love and sincere adoration, I dedicate this book to my beloved parents, Boyd and Maxine. It is because of them I am who I am and all that I will ever hope to be.

To my dearest family and friends whom have closely embraced the joys of sisterhood and sojourned with me the lifetime moments of GFG-Girlfriends' Getaway, I am eternally indebted and always humbly honored.

To those who have walked with me in countless ways of which they may not realize, I truly thank you, love you and greatly appreciate your contributions to my many endeavors in life.

In loving memory of my dear sister and friend Bonita Boatner-Young who shares an eternal piece of my heart. Gone too soon...

—Vikki D

About The Author

*V*ikki **Miller-Walton** is a corporate professional who has traveled extensively for 20-plus years both personally and professionally. Her travels have spanned all 50 U.S. states, 6 continents and numerous countries. As a wife and working mother, having raised a family, while developing lifelong travel friendships, she is convinced that traveling is a key component in the fulfillment of life's journey. It is with this knowledge and wisdom that she is humbly compelled to write this book for your enjoyment, inspiration, and travel enlightenment.

You will find this book to be uplifting and fun, tapping into your inner self and exploring the soulful reasons for taking a GFG—Girlfriends' Getaway. It will potentially push you to step outside your limits and embark on what many women have decided is an important part of their empowerment.

Vikki also recognizes that a GFG—Girlfriends' Getaway can provide benefits that extend beyond not just your personal and professional needs but those of your health and community. With the support of her amazing editor, Peggy Glennie, we want you to enjoy the dialogue and join the GFG—Girlfriends' Getaway club.

Feel free to share your thoughts via email
at gfg_getaway@yahoo.com.

TABLE OF CONTENTS

Preface

As a novice writer, I begin by sharing why I am compelled to write this book. As a woman, I've had the pleasure of sharing my amazing travel experiences with countless women and each discussion was filled with laughter and wonderment. Many have simply said, "You must write a book." I've been told I have to share this knowledge and allow others to engage in the joys of finding themselves, enhancing friendships, and becoming better women as a result of a GFG—Girlfriends' Getaway. "You must show women how to go on a GFG—Girlfriends' Getaway." I honestly agreed that this information needed to be shared and quickly, but how was this possible? With work, kids, family, and all the many obligations of life, I simply didn't have the extra time to devote to writing a book.

Then one day while participating in a work-related training session, our instructor gave us our initial speech assignment centered around effective communication. She required each of us to present an impromptu speech. The purpose of the exercise was to "enlighten" the other participants of the group with our unique communication styles. I chose to discuss my GFG—Girlfriends' Getaway and what inspired me to have the courage to go against the norm. As I passionately discussed how amazing the experiences are of leaving everything behind and focusing on oneself, the joys of the waters of Jamaica, the lovely sounds of the opera in Venice that left me in tears, the shopping expeditions in Las Vegas, I had the other participants—both men and women—bedazzled and in complete and utter amazement. I received one of the highest scores in the class for my presentation. I truly believe it was because I wholeheartedly believed in what I was saying and knew it to be honest and true.

As we went to lunch that day, the instructor pulled me aside and stated simply, "You need to write a book. You have so much to share and you explain it so eloquently that it must be shared with the masses." I didn't have the heart to tell her that I had already thought of writing a book and actually had an outline prepared. I didn't want to expose my weakness in not finding the time to get it done, knowing how important of a topic it is. I began to realize I needed to make some adjustments in my life and get this book into the hands of women who needed it. This instructor confirmed what I already knew. It was time for me to write and complete this book.

Keep in mind, a GFG—Girlfriends' Getaway is not for everyone. Some women are simply not comfortable with going away on vacations without their husbands and families. If you are one of those women, this book is not for you. But for those of you who recognize you spend fifty-two weeks of the year with your family and countless hours at work, if you think you deserve a few days out of the year to maintain some mental sanity, then this book is designed for you.

Also, this trip is not a substitute for your family or romantic getaways with your spouse or significant others. It is simply a supplement for a person you should lovingly embrace and that's you!

This book will provide you with what I believe to be a tool that will take you to places you may have never been before both physically and spiritually. I assure you, a GFG—Girlfriends' Getaway will be well worth the investment in time and commitment to enhancing your personal growth. Trust someone who has embarked on this journey for more than twenty-plus years. Don't get me wrong, it won't change or improve all of your personal situations, but it surely will give you a better understanding of who you are as an individual woman, mother, sister, friend, etc.

This book is going to open the door to many of the wonderful benefits of the GFG—Girlfriends' Getaway. It will explore the benefits to enjoying a GFG—Girlfriends' Getaway through the eyes of women and highlight the positive results. This book is not a traditional travel guide but a girlfriend's soulful guide that uplifts your spirit and explores ways to live life to the fullest. Remember, it's all about the woman in you! I hope this book will empower you to enjoy travels locally, regionally, and globally.

As you read this book, embrace the sincerity and written wisdom and know that I am truly an advocate and supporter of journeys that empower women and also help women to make this world a better place for all to live.

Do not delay. Stop making excuses and do not put off what you know you can do today. Don't be one of those women who say, "I can't do it, it's too hard" or get enthusiastic about a GFG—Girlfriends' Getaway and never follow through with participating in these types of life events. And don't be that woman who procrastinates with sayings such as "I'll wait until I retire" or "once the kids are older." If you don't make the effort, you'll look around and regret missed opportunities.

Remember, tomorrow is never promised. Live for today and plan for tomorrow. Make a GFG—Girlfriends' Getaway a priority. If it's important to you, you'll find a way. This book is a guide to help you find that way by giving you the tools to understand the need and importance. These trips can be a part of the journey of your life, a new life, an enhanced life for you as a woman. And at the end of the day, your family and friends will encourage you to explore these new opportunities once they see the benefits derived from releasing your soul.

Read, receive, and enjoy the thrill of travel over the next twelve chapters and be prepared to share in your own journey. If done right, it will be addictive and satisfying to the soul and you will be saying "I am that girl," the one who embraces life and whom others envy.

Introduction

*T*oday, I'm going to teach you a new acronym. It's "GFG." It stands for "Girlfriends' Getaway!" Yes, GFG—Girlfriends' Getaway is a new term that should become a permanent part of your vocabulary after reading this book. It's time to revolutionize your womanhood and your spiritual self.

A GFG—Girlfriends' Getaway will enhance your friendships and significantly enhance your personal and professional life.

As women, it's important for us to take time for ourselves. Many men have already figured this out. Men, both single and married, take time to enjoy life and the fruits of their labor. Why shouldn't they? They deserve it and so do we! For years many men have taken such trips as hunting, fishing, golfing, sailing, etc. Some take getaways to enjoy an array of sporting events and share bonding relationships with their group of friends that doesn't necessarily include their spouse or significant others or kids. As women, we are comfortable with allowing such activities because it's something that's important to our spouse or significant other. We recognize the importance of ensuring others are happy in their lives and on occasion neglect to carry over that same empathy with ourselves.

And what do we women traditionally do? Stay home with the kids and/or other family members while raising families and working hard inside and outside the home. We rarely, if ever, take the opportunity for a GFG—Girlfriends' Getaway.

Over twenty years ago, my family situation was similar to that of many women I've encountered. At the time, I was a mother of three rambunctious kids aged 3, 4, and 7. I was also holding down a full-time job. I constantly worked and oftentimes brought my work home with me. I've always had a full-time career that required a lot of time, mental endurance, and commitment of the soul. As a result, I rarely found time to simply "breathe." I oftentimes had to share bathroom time with my little ones and remembering those moments often make me smile; however, in the moment it was frustrating. I recall making it a point to ensure that the majority of my spare time was dedicated to the family. Even though my kids were extremely precious and most times incredibly adorable, I would sometimes feel taken advantage of, and quite frankly, used! I was supplying and fulfilling their needs, but who was there to fulfill my needs when I felt neglected? My husband and family circle provided tremendous support; however, there were still gaps that needed to be filled by my own mental fortitude.

On numerous occasions my physical and mental appearance was compromised and I looked raggedy many days and nights. It was not a good look both professionally or personally. As some would say, I was a "hot mess." At times I would even resent motherhood. I was at a breaking point. Can you relate?

I was also absorbed in becoming the perfect employee, perfect wife, perfect mother, perfect friend, and I was forgetting someone. I was not the "perfect me." How is it possible we often forget about ourselves and our personal needs? I was giving entirely too much of my time to others and neglecting myself.

One day when I was overstressed, my dear husband said to me in a soft yet convincing manner, "You need to get away." He suggested that I call my best friend and take a travel getaway to relieve some of the stress that was encompassing my spirit. He recognized the benefits of getting away as he often took golf trips and sincerely wanted me to experience the enjoyment of focusing on myself. What a novel idea and coming from my husband! He made one of the best recommendations of my life. It was a game changer! Thus, began the inception of the GFG—Girlfriends' Getaway!

Now having a family and an intensely challenging job, the very first thoughts coming into my mind were as follows:

- "Can I leave my kids just to go away by myself with friends?"
- "What will people think?"
- "Can we afford this?"

- "Am I being selfish"
- "Am I crazy?"
- "Does this make sense?"

After a few short days of pondering, I relinquished to my own personal desires to obtain a sense of mental sanity and immediately contacted one of my best friends. It didn't take her much time to be on board. Comically, it took her only a few minutes to ask, "Where are we going? I'm all in!" As a mother of four, she was ready to take the leap. She absolutely loved the idea and we began to plot, I mean plan. All the built-up tension of work, family, and stress began to release and I started to begin the process of exhaling.

When my husband initially recommended the idea of getting away, I'm sure he was envisioning a short and simple weekend trip somewhere locally. Living in Northwest Indiana, the logical thought was to travel two or three hours away by car, possibly spending a few days in Indianapolis, Indiana, or even going as far as Lake Geneva, Wisconsin. Ironically, I've never been one to do anything simple; I have a tendency to go big, and big is exactly what I did.

My girlfriend and I decided against a short weekend getaway and decided we were deserving of a full-blown, seven-day, six-night journey for our initial GFG—Girlfriends' Getaway. She and I had to begin experiencing moments in life we never thought of! Seven amazing days in beautiful Hawaii. We stayed in Honolulu and Maui and knew that this was one of those times in our married lives we had found heaven on earth.

Now, over twenty years later, I join other women in groups of all sizes, nationalities, personalities, etc. in traveling the world, from cruises to exotic islands to flying to such diverse places outside the U.S. such as Venice, Paris, Spain, Greece, China, Dubai, South Africa, South America and even Cuba. We oftentimes take trips within the U.S. to major cities like Las Vegas, Los Angeles, San Francisco, Washington, D.C., Seattle, Tampa, Pittsburgh, Napa Valley, New Orleans, New York City, etc. You name it, we'll go. All for the sheer enjoyment of a GFG—Girlfriends' Getaway. I feel very blessed to have traveled to 6 continents, 30-plus countries and all 50 states, and most importantly, I find comfort in knowing the personal benefits of traveling with girlfriends to enhance one's self.

Until my experiences during GFG—Girlfriends' Getaways, I rarely secured moments in time where it was all about me while being laser focused on raising a healthy family and committed to a successful career. Aside from my college years, I had forgotten the pleasure of satisfying my own needs while bonding with women. Those younger years with college friends traveling across the country and abroad had become distant memories as the life of marriage, kids, work, and family commitments took a toll on my soul.

A GFG—Girlfriends' Getaway is truly a spiritual experience that most women will relish for a lifetime. It will require planning, money, and a commitment to enjoy what I promise will make you a better woman, wife, mother, sibling, friend, and colleague.

It's very comical when you casually mention to family, friends, and colleagues that you've taken a GFG—Girlfriends' Getaway. "You went where and with whom?" Assumptions are always made. One colleague casually commented after I had just returned from Madrid. "You and your husband must have enjoyed traveling abroad," she stated nonchalantly. Traveling with my husband is always the instinctive assumption people make.

With a grin on my face and my eyes big and wide, I replied, "I'm afraid you're mistaken. I didn't go with my husband; it was a GFG—Girlfriends' Getaway." She looked stunned and her eyes were filled with amazement.

She softly replied, "A GFG—Girlfriends' Getaway to Europe? I've heard of friends getting away locally for a weekend or maybe to Las Vegas but never to Europe!" Her interest piqued like that of a child who had just walked into a candy shop. She began to breathe and envision what it might be like to experience a GFG—Girlfriends' Getaway and just focus on herself. She then replied in a soft whisper, "Please share every detail." She spoke as if I had a little secret that only she and I could share.

"Oh girl, let me tell you!" And that is why I'm writing this book. I'm sharing the little secrets of a GFG—Girlfriends' Getaway that must be shared with women all over the world.

Another inspiring event occurred while traveling on a GFG—Girlfriends' Getaway in Shanghai, China. We befriended a group of four young Chinese women in their early twenties. They were simply amazed and shocked that we were traveling without our husbands. They also enjoyed our conversations of the many benefits of travel and were inspired. A GFG—Girlfriends' Getaway benefits extends its reach to not just women in the U.S. but around the world. The need for women bonding with shared interests and finding one's self is a common thread for most women.

As women, we are coming upon a revolution and that revolution is the ability for women to enhance our minds, body, and soul. Today's modern woman has been blessed with education, unlimited career opportunities, and tremendous independence. With these blessings comes the obligation to take care of ourselves and enjoy the moments of time we have been abundantly given.

The scenario of wanting to know about the GFG—Girlfriends' Getaway plays itself over and over again. All types of women, including career women, housewives, and even husbands, are increasingly fascinated in hearing about a GFG—Girlfriends' Getaway. The same shock and surprise then become secret discussions that fill women's souls with the thoughts of escaping to the places of their dreams with other women who share that same unfettered passion and desire.

Close your eyes for a brief moment and shut out everything around you. Take a deep breath and begin to imagine yourself on a beautiful beach while listening to the smooth sounds of Sting from your music device. Your skin is glistening from the suntan lotion and the sun is beating down on your relaxed body. You don't have a care in the world. All the drama of your home life and work are drifting away in the ocean. Suddenly you hear a nice hotel worker offer you an exotic drink for your pleasure. You silently sip the drink and as the cool liquid seeps down your throat, you lay back and sigh at the peace of it all. You realize there are no kids climbing on your back, no husband asking you where you moved his socks, no parents, no boss; it's just you and your thoughts. It's all about you.

Now that you have this image visualized, take another deep breath and make a decision that a GFG—Girlfriends' Getaway is for you and you alone. I know you will make the right decision. It will take courage, commitment, and fortitude. You can do it!

As women have evolved in the 21st century, we've become bolder, stronger, more adventurous, and eager to grasp opportunities within our reach. From the fields of business, technology, science, medicine, law, education, and all types of careers, it's now time to take our liberation as women to the next level. As amazing as it sounds, a

GFG—Girlfriends' Getaway is a spiritual journey that propels us into a dimension of sanity from a world oftentimes filled with insanity.

I will also be remiss if I didn't mention the backlash I've received from countless people including female friends who felt I was being selfish and neglectful of my family. Male colleagues expressed their disbelief that my husband "allows me" to do a GFG—Girlfriends' Getaway. Many family members and friends also wondered in disbelief and judgment as to why I would take such an irregular form of travel without my spouse or family. However, as time has gone by, those very same critics have come to wish they had taken the time in their lives to enjoy special moments to enhance their own personal development through travel. Remember your life should never be defined by those who have only a small role in defining and shaping it. Try to consider these trips as an investment in your personal and spiritual being that only you can commit to. It takes grit and courage to not let others dictate your happiness and I'm so very thankful that I was able to withstand the negativity and move forward.

It's also been very refreshing to know that there are many women that have taken the lead and experienced a GFG—Girlfriends' Getaway throughout their lives. We have a sisterhood and when we engage in discussions about travel experiences, there's a common bond. Come join our club.

Let me also add that during another corporate training program, I learned that experiences lead to beliefs that lead to actions that lead to outcomes. I believe that concept is absolutely applicable to a GFG—Girlfriends' Getaway. Enjoying wonderful travel experiences with compatible women will enhance and mold your knowledge and beliefs, leading to improved actions both personally and professionally. The improved actions will surely lead to successful life outcomes that include personal fulfillment, satisfaction, and sheer fun.

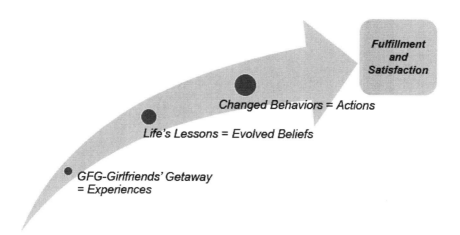

I look forward to sharing the lessons, studies, and journeys that I've enjoyed. I hope it will prepare you for the adventure of a lifetime. Get ready and let's start exploring the purpose of embarking on a GFG—Girlfriends' Getaway.

CHAPTER 1

Why You're Deserving
Of A GFG-Girlfriends' Getaway

"Quit making excuses, putting it off, complaining about it, dreaming about it, whining about it, crying about it, believing you can't, worrying if you can, waiting until you're older, skinnier, richer, braver, or all around better. Suck it up, hold on tight, say a prayer, make a plan, and just do it."

—*Nike*

"Decide once and for all to have an EXTRAORDINARY life."

—*Unknown*

"Travel is one of those things in life that make you richer."

—*Unknown*

CHAPTER 1

WHY YOU'RE DESERVING OF A GFG–GIRLFRIENDS' GETAWAY

WHY?

*W*hy do you deserve a GFG—Girlfriends' Getaway? It's important that you first convince yourself of the deservingness of embarking on a GFG—Girlfriends' Getaway because when you choose to make the right decision for yourself, you don't want to harbor any feelings of guilt or regret. You want to feel confident, committed, and assured that a GFG—Girlfriends' Getaway is the right thing for you. Where do you begin?

It starts with recognizing that as a woman, wife, mother, sister, daughter, friend, coworker, etc. you absolutely have to find time to be *you*. You must take time to enjoy *you*, to exhale and to breathe. A GFG—Girlfriends' Getaway allows you to be selfish and focus on the one that is always with you: *you*. It allows you to step away from all of life's anxieties and pressures and get in touch with your inner soul. You will truly learn to be the best you can be. You will embrace the calmness and inner peace in you. A GFG—Girlfriends' Getaway will most certainly help you achieve the goals you lay out for yourself.

A GFG—Girlfriends' Getaway trip allows you to learn how to love you. And we all know that if you don't love yourself, you can't truly love anyone else nor understand the meaning of love in its abundance, its beauty, and its fullness. Also, keep in mind that old saying, "If mama ain't happy, ain't nobody gonna be happy" or "Happy Wife. Happy Life!" We all know these are true statements. If life's dramas are keeping you from being the genuine, sincere, and wonderful woman you know you can be, then it's time for a GFG—Girlfriends' Getaway. The GFG—Girlfriends' Getaway is like a "restart button" when life presents many challenges. Keep in mind, GFG—Girlfriends' Getaways are not just for married women, women with kids, or those in committed relationships. It's also a great opportunity for single women. These getaways require that you surround yourself with women who express positivity and the love of life.

So let's discuss vacations in general. Most people think of "vacations" as a time to regroup and to get away from it all. So what's the meaning of vacation and why it is important to take them? How is vacation defined? According to the Merriam-Webster dictionary, "vacation" is defined as (1) a period spent away from home or business in travel or recreation, (2) a scheduled period during which activity (as of a court or school) is suspended, (3) a respite or a time of respite from something—intermission, and (4) an act or an instance of vacating.

I would like to highlight a term that is very applicable to women—"respite." As women, we traditionally require a "respite" from our jobs, our partners, our kids, and any other areas in our lives that pull us away from focusing on us. Keep in mind, I am not recommending a permanent "respite" but to incorporate days out of your hectic life to fulfill your personal needs.

A GFG—Girlfriends' Getaway will absolutely provide you with "respite" moments to take time to reflect on life's journeys, foster friendships, and simply have a great time. Getting the appropriate respite will reinvigorate you, give you more energy, and allow for those passionate moments in life to flourish.

As women, when we take vacations with our families, we generally need a vacation from the vacation. I reflect back on my family vacations with the kids, especially the year of the Disney vacation! With sheer excitement, we traveled with three small kids and a mother-in-law, for the infamous Orlando theme parks. I thought I was going to go nuts. We had to do so much, see so much, and be so much that I needed a week to recuperate! As parents, we want to capitalize on all the activities, do everything possible to please our kids. As mothers, we extend ourselves as much as we can for our families and therein lies the need to invest in a GFG— Girlfriends' Getaway for yourself.

Don't get me wrong; I love vacationing with my family and continue to do so. However, let me make it perfectly clear: Vacationing for you is an entirely different ballgame. It's a different experience, hands down!

We women have to overcome our hesitation, misperceptions, and lack of fortitude to take on fulfilling our travel desires. We deserve a vacation with our girlfriends as much as we deserve to take a vacation with our spouse, significant other, and family. Once you confront your concerns, you will truly understand and appreciate the benefits of a GFG— Girlfriends' Getaway.

STUDIES: HAPPINESS, LACK OF VACATIONING, AND HEALTH

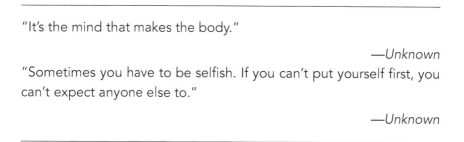

"It's the mind that makes the body."

—Unknown

"Sometimes you have to be selfish. If you can't put yourself first, you can't expect anyone else to."

—Unknown

As women, we go through life taking on challenge after challenge while maintaining households, jobs, and a host of responsibilities. As a result, we sometimes neglect our physical and mental well-being. We become prey to the illnesses that impact our physical bodies along with mental and emotional instabilities. Therefore, it is imperative that we identify ways to minimize disruptions and improve our overall health. Let's examine how vacationing can improve overall happiness, reduce depression, and improve health such as lowering blood pressure, reducing stress, and the anxieties associated with everyday life. Let's also explore how vacationing, including a GFG—Girlfriends' Getaway, can benefit the health of your family and community. Keep in mind, these studies did not look exclusively at women-only getaways; however, it can give you a basic understanding of the benefits of vacationing, social networks and the impact to your body and soul. Let's begin by examining the research.

As we began exploring various studies that focus on the impact of vacationing on happiness, health, and sisterhood, we're going to start by looking back in the mid 2000's. There were research studies done in the Netherlands with a goal of defining the positive outcomes of vacationing on overall happiness and how long the vacation effect lasted. The researchers evaluated 1,530 Dutch adults, 974 of whom took a vacation during the 32-week study period.

The results of the study were published in the journal *Applied Research in Quality of Life*, which found that "vacations do make people happy" and the euphoric effects of which I term "vacation mode" were sustained for at least eight weeks. That's not surprising as we know that when we pull ourselves away from life's commitments to enjoy vacationing, we are going to experience a form of heightened happiness. The research also demonstrated that just the process of planning a vacation provided for a wonderful experience. These results tie nicely into the importance of a GFG—Girlfriends' Getaway. We will further delve into the importance of the planning process along with the financial happiness in Chapter 4, "Decision Made: 'Girls' Night Out' For Planning"; Chapter 6, "Cost and Finances—What to Consider"; and Chapter 10, "Returning Home: Vacation Mode—The Game Changer."

LACK OF VACATIONING

Most people recognize the benefits of vacationing but for whatever the reasons they choose not to take a respite. The rationale for lack of vacationing may include affordability, personal obligations, pressures from the job, etc. According to a recent 2018 survey by Bankrate.com that involved 1,000 American respondents aged 18 and older, 49 percent of respondents said they do not plan on taking a summer vacation. Shockingly, 13 percent of workers with paid time off said they don't intend to use any vacation days provided by their employers.

Expedia releases an annual Vacation Deprivation® study which examines vacation usage and trends across 19 countries. It's a robust study that also highlights vacation metrics such as who takes the most vacation time, attitudes toward vacationing, etc.

The 2018 Expedia Vacation Deprivation® study found that global vacation deprivation is on the rise and 58 percent of workers globally feel they are "somewhat or very" vacation deprived. Gen Z and Millennial's feel the most deprived at 68 percent. Additional studies have found globally 79 percent of workers believe there is a "great deal or a fair amount" of correlation between vacations and overall happiness.

Even employers recognize the importance of ensuring employees utilize their vacation time. Some have policies that require you to use your vacation or lose it. Often, if employees do take vacation, they may also work while vacationing, feeling obligated to remain connected. This impulsive behavior has increased with modern technology. I enjoy traveling to places where Wi-Fi access is limited, or the time zones are significantly different from my workplace. This gives me an excuse to resist working and disconnect while vacationing on the GFG—Girlfriends' Getaway. It's been clearly documented that time away from the stresses of work will make employees effective upon returning.

All of this data is not surprising. This is further evidence supporting the tremendous benefits derived from vacationing with compatible girlfriends.

VACATIONING AND HEALTH

There has been quite a bit of research focused on vacationing and its impact on our health. The Dutch researchers who examined the impact of vacationing on happiness also evaluated the physical health metrics of leisure and vacationing. The researchers surveyed 1,399 study participants who were previously included in studies on breast cancer, cardiovascular diseases, and other conditions. The participants were surveyed on the amount of time they spent engaging in the things they enjoyed. The results found that such leisure and vacationing contributed to more positive emotions, fewer negative emotions, and less depression. People who had more leisure activities "reported more life satisfaction and finding more meaning in life."

Additional evidence of the effects of vacations can be found in a Framingham Heart Study, where scientists searched to identify the key factors that contribute to our well-being. The research included 12,000 men who were at risk of heart diseases and were followed over nine years to see if there were ways to improve their longevity. Among the questions they were asked annually, a few were about vacations.

The analysis of the data showed that the more frequent the vacations, the longer the men lived. The researchers found a positive correlation between more frequent vacations and longer, healthier lives.

As we look more closely at the impact of vacationing for women, a survey of 1,500 women between 1996 and 2001 published in the *Wisconsin Medical Journal* found that the odds of depression and tension are higher among women who get away only once in two years compared with women who are able to travel and leave behind life's challenges at least twice or more per year. McCarty one of the researchers found it shocking that nearly one in five women studied reported taking a vacation only once in six years. The survey revealed that women who took vacations only once in six years thought their home life was more disruptive due to work, felt more tired and exhausted and had less than eight hours of sleep. This pivotal research provides more evidence that vacations provide a break from everyday stressors especially for women.

Also note, there's ongoing focus and conversations around mental health which may be changing how Americans vacation. According to the 2018 Expedia Vacation Deprivation® study, 81 percent of U.S. respondents say they regularly take vacations where their primary goal is "mental wellness," and they overwhelmingly feel that a vacation is a chance to "hit the reset button" on stress and anxiety.

Point blank: Research concludes we can improve our health status by taking the time to vacation and as we explore the bonding of women, you will feel confident in concluding that a GFG—Girlfriends' Getaway can support in strengthening your physical and mental capabilities.

Are you convinced yet you *deserve* a getaway? A respite? Has this discussion spurred that desire that's in you?

STRESS RELIEF: FEMALE BONDING AND EMOTIONAL BENEFITS

"It's my turn to see what I can see, and I hope you will understand that this time is just for me. If living for myself is what I'm guilty of, go on and sentence me, I'll still be free..."

—*Carole Bayer Sager*

Over the past several years, researchers have proven how many health-related issues are due to stress, as well as how various benefits are derived when stress is minimized in our lives. One way to alleviate stress in both our personal and professional lives is to take a respite from the stress-inducing situations and bond with women who have shared interests. A 2018 study released by the American Psychological Association concluded that vacations work to reduce stress by removing people from the activities and environments that they associate with stress and anxiety. As woman we find ourselves in many stressful situations and a GFG-Girlfriends' Getaway is what we need.

A GFG—Girlfriends' Getaway is the perfect solution.

In order to better understand the connection, it's important to explore the mental and physical impact of female friendships. There is true science behind women bonding. One way of examining the science is to measure chemical responses such as oxytocin which is known to have a powerful indirect effect on our health.

Oxytocin is a powerful hormone that acts as a neurotransmitter in the brain. Oxytocin is secreted by the posterior lobe of the pituitary gland. Amongst the many positive things that oxytocin does when triggered and released is that it can regulate social interactions and human connections when people bond socially. According to Psychoneuroendocrinology, positive social interaction and bonding is associated with increased oxytocin along with reduced stress and stress-related hormones.

When oxytocin levels are high, reactions to stress are dampened and stress is less. This is important because it's been reported that increased stress can lead to chronic diseases such as heart disease and metabolic disorders. When oxytocin levels are high, our bodies have been shown to heal faster and obtain better outcomes from wounds.

Psychological Today reports on experts that believe oxytocin is the hormone that also underlies trust and can be an antidote to depressive feelings. Most importantly, oxytocin is believed to be released when women have strong women networks.

This research nicely aligns with studies evaluating the positive impacts of female social networks. Researchers at the Ohio State University and Carnegie Mellon University have shown that people who report strong social networks have immune systems that are stronger and can better withstand various infectious diseases. Studies contend that "social support is the most reliable psychological indicator of immune response."

Additionally, there are studies that show the positive health benefits when people have social support outside of the family. These include improved blood pressure, protective factors in the prevention of dementia and reducing the incidences of depression. Overall, having these types of relationship can lead to positive determinants of healthy aging.

A GFG—Girlfriends' Getaway will bring together your social network of girlfriends with the intent of providing numerous mental and physical benefits. These benefits can contribute to the reduction of stress by the purposeful ability to focus on your needs exclusively. Relieving stress alone can make your GFG—Girlfriends' Getaway become a healthy addiction and an ideal drug for health. These are just a few examples of the mental and clinical benefits of vacationing particularly with your girls. As clinical research advances and evolves, I'm confident that there will be more evidence supporting the importance of embarking on a GFG—Girlfriends' Getaway.

Laughter: Let's now explore laughter and the benefits it provides to healthy living. Laughter is a very important aspect to enjoying life and provides tremendous benefits to healthy living. It is also an important supplement to reducing stress.

I believe it is extremely important to find time to laugh and laugh hard during your GFG—Girlfriends' Getaway. This is one of the many emotional and mental benefits that a GFG—Girlfriends' Getaway will provide.

There is always someone in the group who's a comedian, or funny occurrences just happen during the trip that causes the group to burst into laughter. Make it a point to find and embrace those laughter moments. Some of these moments can be as simple as a girlfriend getting stuck trying to pass through a one-way train turnstile or girlfriends dancing offbeat by the pool. Laughter can help you forget about the mundane experiences of everyday life and the many things that attempt to derail your positive outlook on life.

During a recent GFG—Girlfriends' Getaway, we had a travel companion who told jokes all during dinner. She was so funny that we all anxiously awaited dinner to hear her comic relief. Because we were such a compatible group, the jokes were very appropriate and timely. I can't remember the last time I laughed so hard and was so pleased to have this as an added benefit to the GFG—Girlfriends' Getaway.

According to various sources, laughter triggers the release of endorphins, the body's natural "feel good" chemicals. Endorphins promote an overall sense of well-being and can even temporarily relieve pain. Laughter is also one of the best medicines for your mind and body and should be daily prescribed during your GFG—Girlfriends' Getaway.

Now that you've reviewed some of the physical and health benefits helping to define the need of a GFG—Girlfriends' Getaway, let's now open a dialogue around the soulful importance of a sisterhood and friendships.

SISTERHOOD AND LIFETIME FRIENDSHIPS

I define sisterhood as a relationship that can extend beyond related sisters, and additionally the bonding that occurs between close girlfriends as you share in the experiences of finding yourself. Dictionary. com defines "sisterhood" as an organization of women with a common interest for social, charitable, business, or political purposes. Also, congenial relationship or companionship among women; mutual female esteem, concern, support, etc.

The sisterhood experiences that embody shared interests and social comradery allow for the blending of the minds of women. A GFG—Girlfriends' Getaway provides the perfect experiences to define your sisterhood with friends where you have many common interests and compatible personalities. On a successful GFG—Girlfriends' Getaway, you'll share life's experiences, joys, secrets, tears, and pain. It becomes like a cleansing of the heart, mind, and soul that only women can share. You'll also share life's successes, failures, and finding ways to improve in areas unique to you. You'll find opportunities to build each other's confidence, all the while enjoying an amazing and fun adventure.

It's important to closely assess the bond that women share and the impact to our lifetime personal development. A *Nature.com* study examining our brains and networks found that close friends share coinciding brain patterns. Such research continues to help support the need to have a GFG—Girlfriends' Getaway to enhance your friendships.

Six essential skills to focus on during your GFG—Girlfriends' Getaway:

1. Be a good listener
2. Be transparent and open
3. Jointly celebrate successes in your life and those of your friends
4. Find opportunities to build each other up and support personal development
5. Be true to yourself and be self-aware
6. Identify ways to be a better woman, mother, daughter, coworker, and friend

---

Many men acknowledge the positive benefits of sisterhood experiences having had wives, sisters, aunts, and female acquaintances who discuss and share firsthand their amazing experiences. These are the very same men that find similar bonds with their male friends. Men enjoy various social encounters through activities such as sports, hunting, gaming, and other male-leaning activities. We'll discuss this in Chapter 5, "It's in the Details."

Nonetheless, there are some men who may not understand the need for sisterhood experiences. This can be due to a variety of reasons. It could possibly be due to how they were raised, generational biases, or just simply how they are wired. In some cases, it takes a man or significant other who has a high maturity level and an understanding of the needs of a woman to accept the differences and embrace her travel desires. Although GFG—Girlfriends' Getaways are becoming increasingly more popular, it can be a tough pill to swallow for some men or significant others. Under these circumstances, women may have to continually explain and justify the purpose and value of a GFG—Girlfriends' Getaway. You will also have to emphasize strongly the benefits the spouse or significant other will receive upon your return. A GFG—Girlfriends' Getaway will allow you to enhance your personal relationships and build upon them due to improving your inner self. We'll review these types of discussions in Chapter 2, "Convincing Significant Others."

As you ponder this type of journey, always focus on the important fact that during your GFG—Girlfriends' Getaway, you'll take the time to laugh, talk, eat, sleep, share your soul, and even pray. You may also want to be reckless (in moderation) by spending money on "frivolous" things while being true to yourself. You may want to wear your hair in a different style or dress a certain way that you would never consider doing at home with the kids. However, stay within the boundaries of your spiritual and ethical beliefs. You don't want to do anything you'll regret later. If you want to dress younger than your age, go for it. Be that diva and do it without qualms. Go dancing with the girls even if you may have been a shy dancer and think you don't have rhythm.

Your girls will dance with you, support you, and all of you will laugh the night away.

Additionally, on your GFG—Girlfriends' Getaway, you will overcome some of your hidden fears in the safety zone of your girlfriends who will not be judgmental or critical of areas of weakness. If compatibility is aligned appropriately with the right women, everyone will be supportive of each other and elevate the spirit of womanhood.

Get opinions from your girlfriends on life, love, family, the future, the past, and even work. Share best practices on life skills, makeup, clothes, and all the passionate things that define being a woman. In some cases, you can discuss private female matters because you now have a safe zone of women who most likely will have similar thoughts, ideas and questions. Disagree happily and enjoy each other's company. However, be sure not to get too serious because it can become a vacation downer.

Remember during your GFG—Girlfriends' Getaway, you are finding yourself, enjoying yourself, and sharing the companionship of others who are also finding themselves. This is why it's important to be with women who are extremely compatible. I can't emphasize enough the importance of compatibility. Review your last communications (i.e., text, calls, emails, social media posts, etc.) from your circle of friends and if they are positive and spiritually uplifting, then consider them in the vetting of friends. If not, be cautious. We will further discuss compatibility in Chapter 3, "Who Are Your Girlfriends? Travel Friends."

You will develop lifetime friendships that will be unique during your GFG—Girlfriends' Getaway. You will experience memories that will be permanently etched in your mind. That's why I want these experiences to be the best they can be and this book will give you a few insights to ensure your GFG—Girlfriends' Getaway is maximized to the fullest.

Are you starting to digest the importance of participating in a GFG—Girlfriends' Getaway?

The emotional and health benefits are based upon sound data that suggest vacationing will help relieve stress and provide both mental and physical lifelong benefits. In addition, the sisterhood experiences and bonding provide you a unique opportunity to have the social network of support to strengthen your heart, mind, and soul.

FINDING AND RECREATING YOU

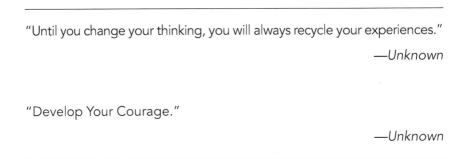

"Until you change your thinking, you will always recycle your experiences."

—*Unknown*

"Develop Your Courage."

—*Unknown*

There are times in life where you must take a moment to find that inner you. Grasping opportunities, taking risks, and stepping outside of your comfort zone requires courage. We also know the importance of exploring the complexities of our mind, body, and soul with others who share a common need. During your GFG—Girlfriends' Getaway, you'll take the opportunity to release yourself from the stresses of life and take a few days to study one of the most important people in your life—you.

Ideally, "finding" yourself should be something you do on an ongoing basis and not relegated to a few days in any given year. This can occur through meditation, religious enlightenment, exercise, yoga, gardening, or a quiet place to reflect. However, in many cases these activities are not enough.

A GFG—Girlfriends' Getaway will take the "finding you" to a different level. You will have positive reinforcement surrounding you from your girlfriends that will make you feel you can accomplish the impossible. Just based on my personal experience, I've identified ideas that led me to want to conquer the world. My friends and I have discussed opening restaurants, starting a clothing and jewelry line, writing books, and a host of other dreams that we ultimately accomplished. The GFG—Girlfriends'

Getaway was a stimulus to our soul and internal drive. We always looked to reach for the stars after a trip. We became re-energized. A GFG—Girlfriends' Getaway provides you with a confidence unlike anything you've ever felt. A GFG—Girlfriends' Getaway will also allow you to improve on your strengths, utilizing them during the planning process as an example. See Chapter 5, "It's in the Details." This book will help you understand the importance of "recreating" yourself.

Now let's look at recreating yourself. We earlier discussed the definition of vacation and now recreation or "recreate," which can occur during a GFG—Girlfriends' Getaway. A GFG—Girlfriends' Getaway can help you improve on areas of faults such as procrastination, hesitation, and fear. On one of my GFG—Girlfriends' Getaway, one of the women in our group had a childhood fear of swimming due to an unfortunate experience of nearly drowning as a child. So during a private boat experience, the women all acknowledged her fears, gently encouraged her to join us all in the ocean of shallow water, and ensured her we had her back. She hesitantly allowed us to take her into the ocean and had tears flowing down her cheeks during the entire experience. These were tears of joy as she overcame one of her greatest fears. It was women who supported her and had her back. Are you ready for such experiences? Life-changing moments?

Now some would suggest a modest day trip or afternoon out with your girlfriends can classify itself as a GFG—Girlfriends' Getaway. Such outings may include a day spa, movies, wine tastings, shopping, etc. However, I would not classify these types of events as an official GFG—Girlfriends' Getaway but more of a girl's outing. Outings with friends are very important and should be a part of your everyday life. However, a GFG—Girlfriends' Getaway is on an entirely different level and will take grit and tenacity. So plan big, aim high, and commit hard. Take your dreams and desires of travel to the next level.

SUMMARY OF WHY YOU'RE DESERVING OF A GFG—GIRLFRIENDS' GETAWAY

"Insanity: Doing the same thing over and over again and expecting different results."

—*Albert Einstein*

Are you ready? Are you getting there? Are you convinced? Are you still hesitant? Are you excited and starting to smile as you think about the people and places that will become memories permanently etched in your heart and mind? Are you contemplating how your mind will broaden and evolve with the experiences of a GFG—Girlfriends' Getaway? Are you ready for this? Is your family ready for this? Well, I believe you are, so let's review what we've discussed. There are four key areas that should solidly convince you that you are deserving of a GFG—Girlfriends' Getaway.

---

1. Happiness, Health, and Emotional Benefits—The scientific evidence supports your GFG—Girlfriends' Getaway.

2. Stress Relief and Laughter—There are positive physical and mental benefits that will result from your GFG—Girlfriends' Getaway. Heightened hormones, stress reduction, and laughter are also amazing health benefits that occur during your trip.

3. Sisterhood and Bonding—The lifetime bonding and friendship developed while sharing this journey with compatible girlfriends.

4. Finding and Recreating Yourself—Grasping the opportunity to take your inner self to the next level. Conquering fears while making a better you and redefining your outlook on life.

So convincing yourself is the first step. Come to terms with it, embrace it, and make it a part of your soul. Once you have made GFG—Girlfriends' Getaway a phrase that nicely rolls off your tongue and plays within your yearly planning, you have won the most difficult part of the challenge and now can officially start the process of participating in a GFG—Girlfriends' Getaway. You can say the phrase with confidence and determination.

You deserve this. As Nike states, *just do it!*

CHAPTER 2

Convincing Significant Others

"It is not selfish to do what is best for you."

—Mark Sutton

"There is only one way to avoid criticism; do nothing, say nothing and be nothing."

—Aristotle

"You've got what it takes, but it will take everything you've got!"

—Unknown

"If you believe it will work out, you'll see opportunities. If you believe it won't, you'll see obstacles."

—Wayne Dyer

CHAPTER 2

CONVINCING
SIGNIFICANT OTHERS

Now that you've convinced yourself, here comes the interesting part: Convincing others why this is an important part of your personal journey in life.

Your spouse or significant other and family members may feel left out and disenchanted by the fact that you want to go on a vacation without them. Many people close to you may take it personally and also convince themselves there's something wrong with the relationship. They simply can't imagine you wanting to embark on an adventure with an exclusive club of women.

Introducing a new concept to families requires methodical planning. You have to be prepared for a discussion about traveling with your girls and its purpose. You have to tackle the discussion head-on with patience, diligence, empathy, and data. It starts by making sure they understand that a GFG—Girlfriends' Getaway is not a replacement vacation but a supplemental vacation. Have them think of a

GFG—Girlfriends' Getaway as vitamin supplements. You get most of your nutrients from food; however, when there are some deficiencies, you add vitamin supplements to ensure you remain healthy. The GFG—Girlfriends' Getaway is a vitamin supplement, a drug that replenishes your mind and soul.

Reassure your critics that they also will benefit and even appreciate your soul-searching adventure with people who support you and share a kindred spirit. Use our earlier discussion points as your guide. Walk through the same benefits you used to convince yourself. All the points are relevant and purposeful.

It's also vitally important that you are fully prepared and armed with answers to many of the complex questions. However, in some situations you may be surprised that your spouse or significant other is very supporting, and the discussion is around planning and preparation. Nonetheless, I'm providing some sample questions that you may have to be prepared to answer. You want to have confidence and authority when you respond. Being aware of these types of questions in advance may give you an advantage and help build your courage.

Here are some sample questions:

"You're going where? With whom?"

"How long are you going to be gone?"

"What about how this makes me feel and the impressions others will have?"

"What about the kids?"

"Are you going through something I don't know about?"

"Are you unhappy?"

"Why are you doing this?"

"It's not safe for women to travel alone. Are you sure about this?"

"Is this something you're going to make a habit of doing?"

"How much is this costing the family?"

"Who are these women you're going with? I'm not sure I want you vacationing with some of them—PERIOD."

Now that you're aware of the importance of being prepared for the host of questions you may encounter, you must now be prepared with top-notch responses. You want there to be no question why a GFG—Girlfriends' Getaway is important to you. You will have to stand tall and strong. Hold you head up high with no shame in wanting to take some time for yourself. You're going to have to be daring in your responses and in some cases brazen.

Here are some sample responses that you may want to share with your spouse or significant other and family members. Keep in mind that all may not apply and of course you have to measure your responses based upon what you know about your spouse or significant other and family members. It's a fun exercise thinking about the discussion. Be sure to practice so that you are seamless in your delivery. Practice will make it perfect. Remember you're selling the concept of a GFG—Girlfriends' Getaway and by the end of the discussion you want to close the deal. The delivery is critical, and you must have a positive disposition, smiling and sincerely listening to your spouse or significant other's questions and concerns. A combative situation is generally not a good way to start a GFG—Girlfriends' Getaway. So, do your best to engage in civility and patience. Try to exercise a little tenderness if it will help you achieve your goal of acceptance and approval. You will become very skilled at responding to others particularly when they ask to participate on your trips.

Here are some sample responses:

- "I want to explore new places and have unique experiences with my friends; this is in conjunction with our special vacation time."

- "I want to enjoy womanly things that you may not be interested in."

- "I want to relax and breathe so that when I return, I will be a better person for you and the family. You know how I sometimes can get in my own head and a GFG—Girlfriends' Getaway will benefit us all."

- "I believe I deserve to spoil myself and get some '"me'" time."

- "It will allow you to spend special time with the kids and family."(Be sure not to burst into laughter at the thought of your spouse or significant other attempting to take on dual responsibilities and I guarantee they will appreciate you even more when you return.)

- Remind them of the things you do for them, their sporting events, their golf trips, the kids' athletic events, family events, etc. This trip is just a small token of their appreciation to you for all the sacrifices you have made for the family.

- Tell them, "If mamma ain't happy, ain't nobody gonna be happy." "Happy wife. Happy life."

- Continue reminding them of the benefits they will enjoy when you come back in the vacation mode and the mental and physical benefits discussed earlier.

- Promise to buy them something special on the trip, especially the kids.

- If they are still not convinced, attempt to get a clear understanding of their concerns and hesitation and find talking points to address those issues. Keep in mind, when dealing with a spouse or significant other, you can always leverage the wonderful reasons why he/she is with you. Don't back down and don't give up.

You know your inner circle best and know what triggers to use to convince them to support you participating in a GFG—Girlfriends' Getaway. Sometimes the adults in your life (such as coworkers or neighbors who have no say in the matter) are harder to convince than your family members. If that's the case, try using this short elevator speech. Simply say the following. "I'm going on a GFG—Girlfriends' Getaway to fulfill my personal desires through life journeys. I have the full support of my family and friends and look forward to sharing the details with you upon my return."

There have also been situations where I've had to simply say, "I'm going on a GFG—Girlfriends' Getaway because I'm a grown woman and I can!" As I like to often say, "That's real talk."

Remember, as you have these conversations, consider the fact that for many of us there are fewer tomorrows than yesterdays and you want to capture as many wonderful opportunities and memorable moments as possible in your lifetime. Don't let others put up roadblocks and certainly don't let fear and apprehension prevent you from enjoying a GFG—Girlfriends' Getaway.

APPREHENSIONS

Apprehension is defined as "worry, unease, misgivings." Feelings of worry about everything from your family's well-being, work, finances, and other life occurrences can cause anxiety. When considering a GFG—Girlfriends' Getaway, these are emotions that are expected. As you know, there are many demands on women. Many of us remember how hard our own mothers worked for the family to ensure we were well taken care of. Now we are our mothers. And for those who are single, you are no less deserving of a GFG—Girlfriends' Getaway due to the challenges you also face on a daily basis.

Convincing a significant other that you and your girlfriends are not going to go wild or that you're not going to run off with a Jamaican stallion may be difficult, but it can be done. Ensure them that you will not be that woman highlighted on social media as one of those "Girls Gone Wild." Reassure them that you're going on a GFG—Girlfriends' Getaway to take the time to redefine *yourself*. Ask them to trust your judgment and respect that you will use discretion where appropriate.

All of us do so much for our kids, family members, coworkers, neighbors, and a host of others that we can be sucked dry into exhaustion and despair. Therefore, you need to take the time to find the girl in you, the woman in you, and enjoy the fruits of your labor. And no matter how nice and relaxing a massage, facial, pedicure, manicure, or good book may be, we need to allow for a GFG—Girlfriends' Getaway to take us to the next level. That's why it's so important to have the GFG—Girlfriends' Getaway become a part of your yearly or biyearly routine. Do your very best to put aside your apprehensions. It will all work out.

In addition to the previous sample questions, I've provided four common concerns known to be problematic to those closest to us. These concerns will have to be addressed initially and may require constant reassurances by you to your spouse or significant other and extended family members. I've provided some examples of responses and solutions that may help alleviate those concerns.

1. Communication—Your family members may feel you will go "off radar" and fail to appropriately communicate.

Solution: Make sure you provide consistent and well-defined communication while on your trip. Utilize your cell phone, text, tweet, email, social media, etc. responsibly. Decide what is most appropriate to assure your family members that you are alive and doing well. Use all types of electronics as a platform to stay connected. Set a schedule so that your family members feel assured you will be accessible. However, be sure not to have them monopolize your time during the GFG—Girlfriends' Getaway. This can be problematic for you and your travel partners. Be very clear on the terms of the communication agreement and this should minimize issues.

2. Costs—For many, this may be the first and biggest concern. Can you justify to your partner how this trip will not cause financial issues?

Solution: Be prepared to discuss simple sacrifices that you will adopt to help cover the costs. This may include working overtime, giving up your morning java, fewer shopping days, etc. Be prepared to provide sufficient accounting of how you will cover the costs. Prepare a cost–benefit analysis for the GFG—Girlfriends' Getaway utilizing some of the points highlighted earlier. Solicit a financial advisor for support where appropriate.

Financial advisors typically carve out travel as part of the family financial planning and health. Be sure to add your GFG—Girlfriends' Getaway to the equation. It may be a tough discussion with your advisor; however, they can help guide and provide assurances that the finances are solid while supporting your decision. In Chapter 6, "Costs and Finances—What to Consider," we will go into greater detail on this topic.

3. Emotional Insecurities—Your partner may exhibit feelings of jealousy, concerns about inappropriate behavior, or just feel abandoned by you leaving. This can cause resistance to your trip.

Solution: This is not uncommon for a spouse or significant other to have insecurities. Recognize these concerns, be mindful, and try to use good judgment in your social media etiquette as not to spur drama that will intensify these insecurities and derail future GFG—Girlfriends' Getaways. Begin working with your spouse or significant other months in advance of your GFG—Girlfriends' Getaway by providing extra tenderness and passion. Providing early assurances and ongoing communication will certainly pay off in the long run. Enhance the levels of emotional support to the highest degree and assure them they will also benefit from your GFG—Girlfriends' Getaway. It will be a win-win for everyone. Make him/her feel secure and loved. What I and others have found is that you will undoubtedly miss them so let them know that. Foster their ego and it will help overcome any challenges.

As the trip approaches, your spouse or significant other may still exhibit some emotional concerns, but they will be milder and manageable. This is most likely the most difficult challenge to overcome. If there appears to be no solution, then you may have to postpone your GFG—Girlfriends' Getaway until your spouse or significant other feels emotionally secure for you to vacation without him/her. This also includes your kids.

> 4. Labor Requirement—Your spouse or significant other is aware that while you're on vacation, they will have additional responsibilities. Whether this is managing the kids, cooking, cleaning or simply handling their own day-to-day activities without your support. There will definitely be increased work requirements. Even those who are skilled in managing the household alone may find they struggle. All types of situations can occur.

Solution: Ensuring they are mentally prepared for this additional labor is essential. There are many ways you can help with the workload while away. It will require precise preparation and planning on the front end of your GFG—Girlfriends' Getaway. Chapter 7 will outline additional details on "Preparations While Away."

Upon addressing all of these issues, you will overcome some of your greatest challenges in participating in your GFG—Girlfriends' Getaway.

MEN AND SIGNIFICANT OTHER EXCLUSIVE SECTION

This section is dedicated to the man or significant other who appreciates their woman and understands the importance of being supportive of his/her woman's growth and personal development. If the love of your life is interested in taking a GFG—Girlfriends' Getaway, it's imperative that you seriously consider your love partner's desires. A GFG—Girlfriends' Getaway will enhance her self-worth and empower her to do things beyond her typical boundaries. Such support from you is long-reaching and will provide you and the family with countless benefits. Look at it as an investment in your relationship and the family structure. It may seem strange to encourage your loved one to enjoy a GFG—Girlfriends' Getaway but your emotional support is critical in order for her to have a successful trip. Keep in mind, her wanting to share time with her girlfriends is not a personal indictment against your relationship. It's not personal. It's all about her. It takes a secure man or significant other to understand and recognize the needs of those close to them.

A GFG—Girlfriends' Getaway will strengthen her mind and body; it will help her be an enhanced partner and friend to you. Although it may appear as a threat or risk as she continues to reinvent herself, remember you both are on this journey together and what's good for her is good for you. When women bond, it involves the blending of the minds that's unique to women only.

All those sayings, "Happy wife. Happy life" and "If mama ain't happy, ain't nobody gonna be happy," are so true. So anything you can do to support her needs and desires is a small gift for all the sacrifices she has made for you and the family. Also, if you push back on her desires, there can be downstream ramifications. Why set the stage for unhealthy drama? Think about it, contemplate, and be prepared to have sincere discussions about it. Let her explain why it's important to her. Have her address any concerns you may have and do so with patience, understanding, and maturity.

If she doesn't have your support and chooses to experience a GFG—Girlfriends' Getaway anyway, it could cause tremendous guilt and ill feelings during her trip and defeat the purpose. So it's important to talk through your concerns and come to an agreement that will ensure a win-win for everyone. You may even be able to negotiate some "goodies" of your choice out the deal. Nonetheless, think about what a wonderful gift it will be to the one you love by supporting her in non-traditional desires and encouraging her to flourish with women who are liked-minded.

If you continue to have concerns, reach out to other partners whose ladies have gone on successful GFG—Girlfriends' Getaways. There are many people who encourage and support their spouse or significant other to take a GFG—Girlfriends' Getaway. Ask and they will share with you the many benefits and pleasures they received upon their loved one's return. There are some men who have recommended a GFG—Girlfriends' Getaway to the wife's surprise. They have embraced the benefits. These benefits begin with what I like to call the "vacation mode" where the spirit of the GFG—Girlfriends' Getaway extends to the entire family upon her return. To learn more about the "vacation mode," review Chapter 10, "Returning Home: Vacation Mode—The Game Changer."

If you truly want to be supportive and demonstrate how special she is, consider the following:

- Provide a financial component for her trip (buy a special piece of jewelry, fun excursion, or some other gift that goes above and beyond the cost of the trip).

- Resist the urge to over-communicate with her during her GFG—Girlfriends' Getaway. Give her space and stand by the agreed-upon communication schedule.

- Share positive updates about the kids with pictures and brief commentaries so that she feels at ease. Please do this in moderation so that she does not feel she's missing out on things and begins to feel guilty.

- Manage all the drama at home and only involve her when absolutely necessary. If you can handle the situation, handle it (and trust me, you can!).

- Upon her return, inquire about her trip, ask questions, and let her tell you all about it. She will appreciate your interest and the opportunity of sharing her special moments will mean the world to her. Even if you get tired of looking at a thousand pictures, sit back silently and let her share.

- Finally, ask her about her next trip and discuss how you believe in her and her dreams and will help support her next GFG—Girlfriends' Getaway.

So men and significant others, I need you to embrace the GFG—Girlfriends' Getaway and be that supportive rock for your queen as she embarks on another unique travel journey. Embrace a mode of understanding the value that a GFG—Girlfriends' Getaway brings to the family unit.

SUMMARY OF CONVINCING SIGNIFICANT OTHERS

"If you do not step forward, you'll always be in the same place."

Now that you've learned how to effectively convince your spouse or significant other of the importance of participating in a GFG—Girlfriends' Getaway, you will have overcome one of your biggest hurdles before embarking on your trip. Assuring and gaining the support of the important people in your life as to the lifetime benefits derived from your participating in wonderful new experiences with girlfriends will make for a much more seamless and fun trip.

In life, we want those closest to us to share in our successes and accomplishments. We need their encouragement and support. Having prepared conversations early on about a GFG—Girlfriends' Getaway will help you convince those who may have some uncertainties. Most importantly, don't be deterred, don't be discouraged, but do speak with confidence and courage. Utilize many of the talking points listed in the chapter and adapt where appropriate.

Remember, be in control of the conversations and release any feelings of apprehension. Provide solutions for concerns and stand firm. You are elevating your game and having the support of your spouse or significant other will provide you with the additional strength to redefine you. You got this.

CHAPTER 3

Who Are Your Girlfriends?
Travel Friends

"Follow your heart, but take your brain with you."

—Unknown

"Surround yourself with the dreamers and the doers, the believers and thinkers, but most of all surround yourself with those who see greatness within you even when you don't see it yourself"

—Unknown

CHAPTER 3

WHO ARE YOUR GIRLFRIENDS? TRAVEL FRIENDS

One of the biggest benefits of the GFG—Girlfriends' Getaway starts with the planning process. The planning process gives you a joy that provides additional enhancements to your GFG—Girlfriends' Getaway experiences.

However, we must ensure that our GFG—Girlfriends' Getaway is a stress-free environment or our goals of rediscovering who we are and having experiences of a lifetime could potentially be ruined.

So once you've convinced yourself and your significant others that you are deserving of a GFG—Girlfriends' Getaway, who will you decide to go with? Will it be your best friend? A sister? A cousin? Coworker? Neighbor? This piece of the puzzle is by far one of the most significant aspects of your trip and is extremely vital to the success of a GFG—Girlfriends' Getaway.

The Merriam-Webster Dictionary defines "compatibility" as "capable of existing together in harmony." Harmony and sisterhood are exactly what you want during your GFG—Girlfriends' Getaway!

Some people just naturally connect as travel companions. Others, not so much. I've traveled in small and large groups and each travel experience is unique in its own right. There is no "perfect" or "magic" number of people to travel with. But compatibility is a major factor whether traveling with one or twelve. Keep in mind, just because you like someone does not mean they are compatible travel companions. If she's not compatible with your style, your likes, your needs, it can be a disaster. And if you travel with more than one girlfriend, the complexities will increase exponentially.

We have certain friends that we do certain things with. We may have a favorite coworker we spend our daily lunch hours with, but we may not want to spend a holiday barbecue with them. Likewise, a friend you enjoy meeting for coffee may not be the best companion for a GFG—Girlfriends' Getaway.

So find girlfriends whom you can bond with, whom you trust to share your personal life's journeys to help you grow, be positive in nature, and be committed to the GFG—Girlfriends' Getaway.

COMPATIBILITY
Examples of Horrible Experiences
While getting information for this book, I've spoken to many women who currently take GFG—Girlfriends' Getaways and they shared their experiences with horrible travel companions. Their bad experiences demonstrated the importance of determining the most compatible girlfriends. In some cases, you're just unsure of how compatible you are with certain friends. However, I'm providing recommendations to assist in identifying how to ensure compatibility. I continue to reinforce the importance of identifying compatible travel companions to ensure a great travel experience.

I recently spoke with a colleague who was taking her very first GFG—Girlfriends' Getaway with a group of 20 women. It was a mixed group of all ages. She did not know any of the women other than her friend who was the organizer of the GFG—Girlfriends' Getaway. She was extremely excited about participating in her very first GFG—Girlfriends' Getaway. They were headed to an exotic location and she needed the break to bring about a calmness in her life after a torrid year at work and in her home life. She had certain expectations of what she desired to experience. However, she would come to learn that her expectations were not in alignment with her girlfriend and travel companions.

Her close friend turned out to be a travel control freak and wanted to make everyone follow a rigorous schedule that included early morning tours, daily exercise routines, and expensive restaurants. When my colleague pushed back on the agenda, her close friend was offended and stated how she had put so much time and effort in the planning and everyone was going to play by her rules! The organizer even made all the room assignments, not considering the individual characteristics of the women.

Needless to say, this was a GFG—Girlfriends' Getaway on steroids! It was going to be an expensive disaster.

I gave guidance to my colleague to be explicit and clear of her objectives and expectations for her next GFG—Girlfriends' Getaway and not bow down to the commands of her travel companions. As a result of her giving in to her friend on this particular trip, she lost all of her ability to savor not only the bonding of women but recreating herself. It also placed her relationship with her close friend in jeopardy. Now she is making significant changes in how she moves forward with future GFG—Girlfriends' Getaways.

Another close colleague discussed her experience with a GFG—Girlfriends' Getaway gone wrong, when she allowed a cousin to attend the trip of four women. Prior to the trip, everyone knew the cousin had an unstable personality, yet they felt compelled to allow her to participate since she was a family member. They also assumed they could manage her behavior. Unfortunately, that was not the case and she ruined the experience for everyone by perpetrating an aura of negativity throughout the trip. Just because someone is family doesn't mean they are always suitable travel companions.

I'm sharing this information with all of you to ensure you don't fall into these situations. I want you to enjoy your GFG—Girlfriends' Getaway to the fullest. Follow your gut. Know your travel companions well. And even though you may be the best of friends, relatives and colleagues, not all travel companions are made equally. As hard as it may be to say no to some people, you have to find a way. It is not up to us to set aside our own desires in an attempt to constantly please others. That's a recipe for disaster. Always remember a GFG—Girlfriends' Getaway is for you to find yourself and bond with friends where there's compatibility. You are not on vacation to entertain other people. That's considered a family vacation. If you're one of those people who have difficulty engaging a variety of personalities, it may make sense to vacation alone or with your immediate family who may have a higher tolerance for your personality style.

Successful Experiences

While participating in a GFG—Girlfriends' Getaway to Dubai, I was surprised at the uniqueness of the trip. It included more than 60 people and a close inner circle of family and friends. The trip integrated a group of people with different personalities and passions, yet we respected each of our own individual desires to do our own thing during the trip. For example, if you weren't interested in going on the tours, there was no pressure from anyone. I also like to work out and was able to incorporate that into our daily routine without hindering other travel companions. Other smaller groups took side trips that were of their own interests, all so that everyone could be fulfilled by their GFG—Girlfriends' Getaway. It was easier than expected and no drama.

Knowing in depth your travel companions and how to leverage that relationship into an amazing experience is by far the greatest benefit of a GFG—Girlfriends' Getaway.

Therefore, I've provided a GFG—Girlfriends' Getaway *Compatibility Assessment of Girlfriends* for you to use to determine if your travel companions are appropriate with your style of travel. You should not begin planning a GFG—Girlfriends' Getaway until you have identified the right travel companions.

Keep in mind, the points listed are just suggestions and a guide for you to use to identify the most appropriate travel companions. Also consider a weighted scoring system to determine who is most compatible. This might seem strange but considering the time, cost, and commitment required to have a successful GFG—Girlfriends' Getaway, it's a critical exercise to complete.

Let me be clear, there will be some differences in compatibility; however, there should be more similarities than differences, so it's important to weigh those factors.

I've also been asked about traveling on a GFG—Girlfriends' Getaway with women you don't know. Those situations I wouldn't necessarily recommend as your first option for several reasons. You want to take the opportunity to foster and enhance existing relationships with girlfriends that have had some sort of footprint in your life. It will provide a sense of comfort and security. However, if for whatever reason that's not possible, then traveling with women you don't know can also be an experience of a lifetime as I know several women who have done it. Keep in mind there's risks and be prepared for wherever the situations land.

So, let's explore the important aspects of compatibility by assessing key characteristics.

COMPATIBILITY ASSESSMENT OF GIRLFRIENDS

    1. Defining the Relationship: Start with defining the relationship of the companion—family member, close friend, neighbor, college friend/sorority sister, work colleague, neighbor, casual acquaintance, single women vs married women, etc. Be careful with mixing and matching of different relationships, for example, a work colleague with family members.

2. Demographics: Identify variations in age, nationality, religion, income, profession, and the health of travelers. Millennials and Baby boomers? Always consider the dynamics of the group.

This is very important because these dynamics are critical in determining the boundaries, activities, and tolerance level for the GFG—Girlfriends' Getaway. For example, if religion prevents someone from drinking alcohol and members of the group are active drinkers, there may be conflicts. Another example is the social media habits of Millennials vs Baby boomers. They can be very different. Or maybe the younger generation may want to hang out at clubs, and you want to chill and read a book. There can certainly be a disconnect. If you're aware that there may be differences, there should be no problems.

3. Diversity: I am a big proponent of diversity in the GFG—Girlfriends' Getaway travel group; however, there needs to be a nice mix and an understanding that there may be differences.

4. Financial Compatibility: Ensure everyone aligns around finances. More discussion on this in Chapter 6, "Costs and Finances—What to Consider."

5. Personality Characteristics: We all have our own unique personalities and some personalities are more compatible than others. Our personality type can include being extroverted, introverted, etc. and we need to be mindful of those participating in a GFG-Girlfriends' Getaway. We'll further discuss personality categories and traits later in the chapter.

Additional Travel Assessments of Personal Styles and Traits

- Are you a morning or night person? Are they?

- Also, consider the cleanliness of your travel partners. If you carry Lysol and sanitary wipes in your purse, it's important your travel partner is not filthy. It will drive you crazy. Try your best to assess those very important traits and be prepared to adapt as appropriate. Are you messy or meticulous? Be self-aware. Are they? How much can you tolerate?

- Are you frugal or excessive in spending? Luxury versus economy traveler?

- Do you hate or love to shop? Do you like crafts, gardens, cooking?

- Vegetarian, food snob? Alcohol drinkers vs nondrinkers?

- Do you love city action like New York City vs hiking in the mountains of Utah? Maybe you're flexible and enjoy all types of vacation. You just need to be sure that your travel partners share similar interests.

- Are you in good physical shape or need some encouragement to work out?

- Are you an experienced traveler or novice?

- Are you consistently on time or late? It's important that you're honest with yourself and your travel behaviors.

- Are you a timid person, introverted, an aggressive type "A" personality, extroverted, spontaneous, risk taker, or conservative?

- Do you snore? Talk or walk in your sleep?

Dig deep in understanding the personal interests of your travel companions. For example, an experienced shopper or wine connoisseur may not be pleased with walking in gardens or doing arts and crafts.

On the same token, a person who loves to see nature and national parks may not want to waste time on shopping. Or you may have people who love to do it all. Nevertheless, the key to a GFG—Girlfriends' Getaway is that you should be able to do whatever *you* like to do.

The only mandatory agenda you should have to follow is your own. If you don't want to go to the mall, don't go! If you don't want to go on the nature trip, don't go! Do what relaxes you and makes you happy. Do your best to try to find ways to align your interests with those of your travel partners but don't feel obligated. Keep in mind, if there are some differences, it's ok. This is your trip and all about you. All decisions should be a part of the GFG—Girlfriends' Getaway planning process, which we will discuss in Chapter 5, "It's in the Details."

These are just a few examples of commonalities you will need to discuss with your girlfriends while examining yourself to ensure compatibility. I'll continually emphasize the importance of self-awareness and emotional intelligence when defining compatibility.

Let's look at how these personal styles and traits apply to your GFG—Girlfriends' Getaway.

If you are a morning person and want to get up very early to start your day and you happen to travel with people who like to stay out late and sleep in, there could potentially be a conflict, particularly if it's your roommate. However, if you are aware of the differences at the beginning of the journey, you can make adjustments in the planning. Possibly make alternative travel arrangements such as a single room so as not to disturb others. Planning and awareness are key.

One of my close travel companions likes to sleep in because she has to get up very early for her job. She does not want an alarm clock to wake her up during our GFG—Girlfriends' Getaway. I completely understand; however, I like to get up early to work out. So, I quietly get up and make sure not to disturb her. I appreciate not having to make early plans so that I can get a good work out in. She appreciates the ability to sleep as long as she likes. So, although we have differences of styles, we have learned to adapt. It has allowed for our travel experiences to be seamless and relaxing. The compatibility score is high.

Compatibility assessments are an absolute must prior to embarking on a GFG—Girlfriends' Getaway. Now let's further examine the personality traits of travelers that embark on a GFG—Girlfriends' Getaway.

"WHO ARE YOUR GIRLFRIENDS?" TRAVEL FRIENDS' PERSONALITY CATEGORIES

According to psychology experts there are five personality traits also commonly known as the five-factor model (FFM) and the OCEAN model.

1. Openness to experience (inventive/curious): Appreciation for art, emotion, adventure, unusual ideas, curiosity, and variety of experience.

2. Conscientiousness (efficient/organized): A tendency to be organized and dependable, show self-discipline, act dutifully, aim for achievement, and prefer planned rather than spontaneous behavior.

3. Extraversion (outgoing/energetic): Energy, positive emotions, surgency, assertiveness, sociability and the tendency to seek stimulation in the company of others.

4. Agreeableness (friendly/compassionate): A tendency to be compassionate and cooperative rather than suspicious and antagonistic towards others.

5. Neuroticism (sensitive/nervous): The tendency to experience unpleasant emotions easily, such as anger, anxiety, depression, and vulnerability.

These align nicely with the behavioral and personality categories of travelers' outlined below. Many of you can identify with some of these behavioral and personalities traits when you reflect on your relationships with your girlfriends. You may have different terms but hopefully you'll understand the importance of being aware of the behaviors and personalities of your travel companions when embarking on your GFG-Girlfriends' Getaway. Let's further explore the behavior and personality categories below.

The "Backpacker"—This travel personality comfortably allows you to plan everything, do everything, and manage all the logistics of the vacation. They rely on you and others to handle every situation and they simply sit back and ride you (like a backpack) and they like to wait for the outcome. They don't necessarily volunteer to assist in the overall planning and simply let others in the group shoulder most of the responsibilities. They may also not speak up. Most GFG—Girlfriends' Getaways have "Backpackers" and it's not a problem as they tend to "go along to get along."

Be sure to find ways to engage these people and delegate responsibilities. They may remain quiet as the group delegates, so it's imperative you purposely involve them. Have someone be responsible for air travel, someone else for tours, someone else managing the lodging, etc. This will minimize having too many backpackers. We'll further discuss the delegation of assignments in Chapter 5, "It's in the Details."

The "Timid"—Rarely travels, inexperienced, and needs a lot guidance during the GFG—Girlfriends' Getaway. This travel personality may also be afraid to take risks and is more conservative in their travel options. You will have to encourage them to step outside their comfort zone and push the limits. They agreed to do a GFG—Girlfriends' Getaway so be sure to guide them to enjoy it to the fullest.

The "Opportunistic"—These travel personalities are looking to "showcase their travel experience" via social media and will take every opportunity to expose every experience the group encounters from the food selections to someone tripping and falling by the pool. Don't try to discourage their experiences but be extremely clear with them that either they are an active participant in this getaway or not. Everyone has their own way of building up their personal ego and self-esteem. Respect and acknowledge what works for each traveler.

In Chapter 9, "The Vacation," we will discuss in greater details the rules of engagement for social medial activities.

The "Matter of Factly"—Be wary of the "matter of factly" travel personality. They can potentially derail the positive experiences of the GFG—Girlfriends' Getaway. No matter how much planning and organizing is done, they find some reason to complain without providing any solutions or effort. You should also be able to weed out these types of travelers as you go through your compatibility scoring.

The "Take Charge"—These are travel personalities who like to take ownership of the vacation for you and the entire group. In some cases, this can be helpful because they will handle crucial situations, but in some situations, they may want to apply intense influence of their wants and desires over the entire group. Be sure to find ways to rein in these personalities as not to cause conflict and drama. I must admit I can sometimes fall into this category and continually have to stand down as to not to ruin the GFG—Girlfriends' Getaway for the group due to my own type "A" personality and aggressiveness.

The "Supporter"—These are the type of travel personalities you definitely want to be a part of the group. They tend to be mediators and support the efforts of the planner. They try not to cause waves and will work to be harmonious.

The "Experienced"—Experienced travelers are invaluable and provide tremendous insights to the vacation. Although sometimes shunned as "know-it-alls," they help in ensuring the vacation is a success. Try to recruit a handful of these folks if possible.

The "Wild and Reckless: Independent Spirit"— I would be remiss not to mention those who are "out there." There are always those girlfriends who "go off the rails" and want to do their own thing. This is not to be scorned but managed. Keep in mind these are grown women paying their own money to vacation, so just be aware of their goals and be mindful of their intentions.

The "Financially Challenged"—These are folks who barely pulled the funds together to take on the vacation. They are going to be limited in their ability to participate fully. Be aware and sensitive to this and cut them some slack. Have empathy and look for economic ways to ensure they can fully enjoy their vacation while not sacrificing the enjoyment of the entire group.

The "Visionary"—Are you a person that looks at a glass half empty or half full? These types of girlfriends add a refreshing flavor to the group. They have an inviting spirit and tend to always smile. They look for unique opportunities to explore and bring a broader view to the bonding of women.

So, let's examine how these behavioral and travel personalities play out in a real world GFG—Girlfriends' Getaway. During a recent GFG—Girlfriends' Getaway trip to Cabo San Lucas, Mexico, I broke away from my girlfriends and decided to spend some quiet time in the hotel Jacuzzi. To my surprise, while alone chilling in the hot tub, there were five college friends on their annual GFG—Girlfriends' Getaway. I thought, "How exciting!"

The women joined me in the hot tub and we immediately became engaged in conversation. I was fascinated by their seamless interactions and was able to observe their similarities and differences. In my opinion, they scored high on compatibility and personality styles.

The five women were a diverse group of friends of multiple ethnicities and from various regions of the U.S They also were all shapes and sizes. One was single and a corporate executive. She was the "take charge" and "experienced" travel friend in the group. She traveled extensively both professionally and personally. She also managed the financial purse strings. One of the women was single and involved in a new love interest. She was the "opportunistic" one in the group. Before I knew it I was a friend on her Facebook page. There was the married wife with no kids who was the "wild and reckless" friend. She would actively engage with the other resort guests and would pull people into our conversations. The other two were married with kids. Of these two, one was a "visionary." She always had something positive to say about the group and life experiences. The other one was the mediator of the group, effectively handling all of the awkward comments and situations. Their GFG—Girlfriends' Getaway was the perfect mix of personalities and compatibility.

Their experiences and expectations for the GFG—Girlfriends' Getaway were slightly different from mine, as life's journey makes the trip take on different meanings for each person. However, the converging of five women who were experiencing marriage ups and downs, career swings, child-rearing activities, and even the complexities within their friendships met all the criteria for embarking on their GFG—Girlfriends' Getaway. Not surprisingly, they all admitted that they were going to walk away from Cabo feeling stronger as women, mothers, spouses, and friends.

They even handled conflict well as one of the single friends with a new love interest was asked to spend some time alone due to her love interest causing some drama. The "supporter" handled the situation and ensured it didn't cause drama during the GFG—Girlfriends' Getaway. The girlfriends collectively knew exactly how to appropriately manage the situation.

The girlfriends shared with me their excursion experiences and the funny situations throughout their trip. The laughter we all enjoyed by sharing stories and the memories we collected were all quite fulfilling. And although I had just met these amazing women, I was excited to be asked to join their next GFG—Girlfriends' Getaway.

Now looking more at personality traits, which of these are you? I've highlighted self-awareness and emotional intelligence on a few occasions. In the business world, emotional intelligence and self-awareness are incredibly important for success. This refers to being emotionally aware of one's own behaviors and personality traits and the impact these traits have on others and your performance. It also helps define how you approach and deal with a variety of situations. These same traits are critically important when embarking on a GFG—Girlfriends' Getaway. Being self-aware and acknowledging the personalities of yourself and your travel partners will aid in ensuring you have a wonderful experience.

Keep in mind, you may exhibit a combination of these personality traits so be self-aware. Find your girlfriends who align with your strongest personality traits and it's ok to have a variety of personalities because diversity adds to the fun and uniqueness of your GFG—Girlfriends' Getaway. The important point is to be aware upfront and pull together a group that's compatible.

SUMMARY OF COMPATIBILITY OF TRAVEL FRIENDS

"Be picky about who you keep around you. Personalities, words, and traits do rub off."

—Unknown

I cannot begin to overemphasize the importance of traveling with the most compatible girlfriends possible. Just like in any relationship, compatibility is terribly important and more so when taking a momentous journey such as a GFG—Girlfriends' Getaway. We are very unique in our own styles, personality traits, etc. As a result, we need to ensure that those who we surround ourselves with during our GFG—Girlfriends' Getaway are a good fit.

We have to be acutely aware of our own personalities and styles along with having emotional intelligence for those girlfriends around us. Embracing and recognizing the importance of compatibility will eliminate horrible experiences as discussed in the chapter. Closely look at the companion compatibility assessment and use it as a guide to understand the behavioral and personality types of travelers' you will be surrounded by during your GFG—Girlfriends' Getaway. Pull together a group that is a great mix and you're on your way to a wonderful experience.

CHAPTER 4

Decision Made –
"Girls' Night Out" For Planning

"You don't have to be great to start, but you have to start to be great."

—*Zig Ziglar*

"Maybe it won't work out. But maybe seeing if it does will be the best adventure ever."

—*Unknown*

"I love when conversations and energies just flow. Not forced. Not coerced."

—*Unknown*

"Stop trying to make everyone happy. You aren't chocolate."

—*tobymac#spesaklife*

CHAPTER 4

DECISION MADE—
"GIRLS' NIGHT OUT"
FOR PLANNING

*P*re-planning for your GFG—Girlfriends' Getaway is proba-
bly one of the most important aspects of the trip. I strongly
recommend scheduling a "Girls' Night Out." You can never
be overly prepared. We've learned through our travel experiences
that effective preparation and planning is equally as important as the
implementation of the trip. Interestingly, studies indicate that there
are tremendous benefits to a vacation beginning with the planning of
a vacation. Effectively planning for your GFG—Girlfriends' Getaway
will allow for a seamless experience, minimizing drama and ensuring
the group is on the same page. It will allow for the appropriate delegating of responsibilities and setting expectations. This starts with the
"Girls' Night Out" of planning to accomplish this goal.

The "Girls' Night Out" can be held at a coffee shop, a friend's house, a
restaurant, or some other cool venue. We also develop a "text group"

dedicated for the women to keep up the hype and communicate both pre- and post-GFG—Girlfriends' Getaway. Make sure the venue allows you to actually get work done so you're not just chilling. In most cases, you may need more than one night out. Keep in mind, some of your girlfriends may not live locally and require the group to be creative in the planning. This may require utilizing technology to bring the group together. Be sure to make the planning fun, no matter the format. Most importantly, allow for ample time to plan and make it a nice event.

The planning and the anticipation are part of the joy of the GFG—Girlfriends' Getaway. My friends and I mark our calendars for monthly teleconferences and live meetings leading up to the date of departure.

It's extremely important that you schedule regular "Girls' Night Out" events for preplanning because it allows for the delegation of responsibilities and the setting of goals, objectives, and purposes for your trip. Does it sound like a business meeting? Yes! It's important that everyone is on the same page for what each of you hope to gain from this wonderful adventure. It also holds each of you accountable for various action items. The "Girls' Night Out" for planning will eliminate all the responsibility falling on one person. Be prepared to roll up your sleeves and get to work. We will discuss in Chapter 5, "It's in the Details" the importance of delegating responsibilities.

Just think about family vacations. In most cases, either mom or dad coordinates all the details and plans for the entire event. In a GFG—Girlfriends' Getaway, you have the help and resources of the entire group. That's what makes it even more of a wonderful experience. The burden doesn't always fall on one person's shoulders. I've been in situations where I've been the primary planner and organizer, which is a heavy load for one person to bear. When everyone shares in the planning process, they take on shared ownership. This way all the personality peculiarities of the girls can come to light and be adjusted for. Make sure you don't put yourself in that position of being the lone wolf and delegate appropriately.

Finally, during the "Girls' Night Out" be sure to relax and have fun. Be sure to share your excitement and your expectations for the trip.

Share some of your concerns about leaving your loved ones so that you can support each other if necessary. Laugh and enjoy as this is the beginning stage of your GFG—Girlfriends' Getaway. Keep in mind, this is part of the sisterhood that you are building.

The "Girls' Night Out" should ideally occur approximately 6–12 months prior to the trip. This gives everyone plenty of time to research and to meet for regular "Girls' Nights Out."

SUMMARY OF GIRLS' NIGHT OUT

"By failing to prepare, you are preparing to fail."

—Alan Lekein

In summary, a "Girls' Night Out" is the perfect opportunity to begin to get a taste of what your GFG—Girlfriends' Getaway is going to be like. It's a small precursor to working with your girlfriends as well as having your family spend some time with you away, if only for a few hours. As we discussed, studies have shown that simply planning for a vacation carries numerous benefits. Have fun planning and building up the anticipation of the GFG—Girlfriends' Getaway.

During a "Girls' Night Out," you will also have an opportunity to assess who's on time, who's organized and prepared. This will set the standards for what's going to be a trip of a lifetime.

CHAPTER 5

It's In The Details

"A goal without a plan is just a wish."

—Unknown

"Planning is bringing the future into the present so that you can do something about it."

—Alan Lekein

CHAPTER 5

IT'S IN THE DETAILS

hether you and your girlfriends are embarking on a weekend GFG—Girlfriends' Getaway or preparing for a longer trip, there are some things you do not want to leave to chance. Effective and efficient planning and taking a good hard look at the details will ensure your GFG—Girlfriends' Getaway is an experience of a lifetime.

As we discussed, it's imperative that you and your travel companions plan together and don't place all the work on one or two people. Delegate responsibilities and be reliable when given assignments. Contribute where appropriate and enjoy the experience. It truly is fun to plan an adventure. There should be modest give and take; however, if the compatibility factors are high then it should not be an arduous process. Each of us have specific things that we require and need when embarking on a GFG—Girlfriends' Getaway. Do your best where appropriate to accommodate the entire group and identify areas where there can be compromise if there's a disagreement. There have been circumstances where I've had to compromise and knowing in advance made it tolerable and didn't hinder the GFG—Girlfriends' Getaway. It's those unknown circumstances that cause drama and confusion. We will discuss drama in Chapter 8, "Disruptor Situations—No Drama Mama."

Let's highlight the key factors to consider during the planning process.

TIMING: WHEN DO YOU GO? HOW LONG?

When are girlfriends most stressed? During the holidays, during summer break, winter months? When determining when to do your GFG—Girlfriends' Getaway, identify a timeframe that's most suitable for the entire group. Make sure the timing doesn't conflict with other family and work commitments. The trip should occur during periods that will allow you to return well rested and prepared to conquer many of life's experiences. Most certainly, consider the seasons of the location as that will play heavily on the costs, outcomes, and experiences.

For example, if you have educators in your group, a summer timeframe may work best if it doesn't conflict with family vacations. Or if you're planning a New England road trip, the fall months are perfect. Off-season travel may be more affordable but Paris in the summer is an experience of a lifetime. So, identifying the time of year most suitable for the group will play a critical role in dictating the location.

When determining the time frame of the trip, make sure the length is not too short or too long. Both can be problematic. Too short of a GFG—Girlfriends' Getaway can leave you feeling slighted and disappointed. As mentioned earlier, if you're only able to get away for a weekend, then plan appropriately. If you have more time, then go for it.

TYPE OF TRIP: THE DESTINATION

Once you've completed the compatible profiles of your traveling companions, you can begin to identify the type of trip. There are countless types of vacations to fit your personalities and interests. Vacations can consist of customized tours or adventurous tours. You can relax at exotic beach resorts or plan for international excursions. Do you want to volunteer? Do a road trip? Do lots of hiking and other outdoor activities? Do you want luxury or a cultural authentic location? You name it and it's out there.

This type of decision making will require some compromise from the group as everyone has ideas on what their bucket list of travel looks like. However, if you're a compatible group of girlfriends, you will come to a common consensus. Also note that the budget and costs will play a key role in the deciding your trip's location and length. Be sure to expand your horizon; consider exploring places none of you have ever been. Keep your options open.

Location Compatibility: If your group of women love to shop, you have to consider a location that satisfies the group. Places such as New York and Paris or metropolitan areas with lots of shopping options are ideal. If your group is not interested in shopping but would like to just have intense relaxation, then places with a beach such as the Caribbean or Florida would be perfect, or even a luxury resort where you can have days and nights by the pool or ocean side, which can do wonders for the soul. Does your group want to educate their minds? Places like Washington, D.C. with the Smithsonian museums can suit the needs of the group. What about a group of women who want to just party? Then, of course, Las Vegas is the place to go. More active women may want to explore the Pacific Northwest with outdoor activities that fill their days and nights. A cruise, land trip, it's all an option. Levels of taste should also match. Remember it's all about you, your girlfriends, and shared desires. Take your imagination to the fullest and have the group decide.

If you recall in Chapter 3, "Compatibility—Travel Friends," we discussed how the compatibility of travel companions will help define the location. It is vitally important that you know your girlfriends and their specific needs. If not, you may find that people are frustrated and not pleased with the GFG—Girlfriends' Getaway. Let me reiterate, you must be clear on everyone's interests, including *yours*, for the GFG—Girlfriends' Getaway to be successful. It's ok during the trip if their objectives differ from yours. That's what's wonderful about these trips. Everyone can independently do their own thing and connect as desired. When people begin to impose their own desires upon you, that's when you may have to re-evaluate your travel companions and their compatibility.

HELP PLANNING: TRAVEL AGENT/CUSTOMIZED TOUR GROUPS/TRAVEL CLUBS/PLAN YOURSELF

Although this book is not a travel guide, I've provided some insights on how to get started. One of the first questions people ask is, "Where do I begin?" If you are a novice traveler along with your group of girlfriends, I would recommend working with a travel agent or an experienced traveler willing to dedicate their time in assisting you.

As you begin to identify places, you will be surprised by the suggestions and input people who have already visited such locations are willing to share with you. People will make suggestions on locations, hotels, restaurants, sightseeing, and even offer to have you connect with their friends in the location of interests. Be very open to receiving advice from a variety of experienced people to gain as much information as you can, ensuring you're maximizing resources. You'll be pleasantly surprised by how wonderful people's advice on vacationing can be in the planning and the success of your GFG—Girlfriends' Getaway. I often rely heavily on word of mouth advice from friends and colleagues. It's been priceless!

In the Details Sample Checklist

- When and where are you going?
- How much are you willing to spend? Budgets

- How are you planning to get there? Mode of transportation?
- What activities do you want to experience?
- Logistics (what to wear, packing, etc)
- Rules of engagement
- Assignments and time frame for completion of duties
- Lock in dates for additional "Girls' Nights Out."
- Support each other if there are challenges such as financial, apprehensions, etc.

When we began our initial GFG—Girlfriends' Getaway, we utilized a travel agent to provide us with guidance, suggestions, and reassurances. At that time, when travel technology was in its infancy, the travel agent kept us alert to the best deals available and also kept us abreast on options we may not have considered. If the group chooses to use a travel agent, my experience has dictated that the agent needs to have plenty of travel knowledge, particularly about your destination of choice, and understand the specific needs and desires of the group. We've also contracted with third-party assistance when renting beach homes, scheduling tours, etc. Again, these are just examples where hiring services may assist.

For many of our trips, my travel companions and I planned our trips on our own and we chose not to use a travel agent. We learned to effectively delegate responsibilities.

We utilized multiple printed travel guides on the locations we were visiting. Years ago, we could easily walk into a bookstore and find numerous travel guides on the locations we were considering. Today, you have countless web and app-based resources to provide information as well as assist in the researching of the locations. We now leverage all the tools available such as travel apps, reviews, videos, etc. I'm amazed by how technology has enhanced the travel experience by making it easier and more accessible. The language translation apps alone have changed our travel experiences while traveling internationally. Whether the group utilizes a travel agent or plans independently, it's always good to do your own research.

Be sure to have documentation, which includes your planned itineraries and schedules, lodging, etc. for everyone as a convenience. Someone will have to own this process. Identifying someone to maintain the itineraries and pull together all the logistics is important. Even if you're using an agent, you will still need to have a logistics point person. So, let's begin discussing in greater details the importance of delegating responsibilities.

DELEGATION OF ASSIGNMENTS

In order to ensure that all the bulk of the work doesn't fall on one or two people, it's important to effectively delegate responsibilities where appropriate. Keep in mind, everyone will not be required to carry a heavy load. However, most of the travelers should shoulder some of the pre, during, or post trip planning work. If most of your girlfriends take some ownership in the planning and orchestrating of the GFG—Girlfriends' Getaway, it will ensure a successful trip. This will also allow for diverse viewpoints on options while alleviating unnecessary burdens upon a few.

When delegating assignments, be sure to decide who is responsible for what based upon an individual's passion and capability to accomplish their assignment. For example, someone may love history and architecture. That person would be ideal at arranging tours for the trip. Someone else may fly often and would be perfect to identify affordable air travel and monitor airline policies. If someone is a good driver and navigator, let them be responsible for transportation during the trip. If someone loves to shop, let them be responsible for identifying the best shopping locations. The financial person in the group can manage the budget, be the treasurer, and identify the appropriate financial needs for the trip. If someone is multilingual, lean on them as the interpreter for the group while in a foreign country. For someone such as myself who is very particular about lodging and insisting on certain amenities, it is most appropriate for me to oversee the housing arrangements. Also, keep safety protocols as part of the planning and delegating.

Utilize people's unique skillsets and it will make for an enjoyable experience for everyone. Be sure to hold each other accountable for their assignments. No excuses such as "I was busy with the job, the kids," etc.! Everyone is busy and your trip must be a priority. Your girlfriends are relying on you and you are relying on them. The upfront planning will ensure success of the GFG—Girlfriends' Getaway so you can't drop the ball.

Make note that even when using a travel agent and third-party services, there are still areas for delegation, so assign appropriately.

COMMITMENT

When you make a commitment with your girlfriends to participate in a GFG—Girlfriends' Getaway, be sure to be committed. We all recognize that life happens; however, there have been too many situations where girlfriends get excited and make commitments to participate and then pull out.

When you pull out on the group, it can cause all types of disruptions and issues. Be upfront early with your girlfriends if you think there could potentially be challenges with you participating. Be diligent in confirming your work schedules, child care arrangements, etc. There's nothing more frustrating than girlfriends committing both financially and emotionally to a GFG—Girlfriends' Getaway and then bailing at the last minute. This can ruin relationships. Therefore, be as upfront and honest as feasibly possible during the early stages of planning if you believe there may be some challenges. If an unfortunate situation occurs prior to the trip, be expedient in notifying the group so that alternative planning can occur. It will be the best for all.

SUMMARY OF IT'S IN THE DETAILS

"Plan your work and work your plan"

—Unknown

Throughout our lives we recognize the importance of proper planning. Without effective planning both professionally or personally, we can find ourselves in unfortunate situations that could have been avoided. It's equally as important when planning a GFG—Girlfriends' Getaway. If you plan the details to the best of your abilities, you can sit back and relax as your trip will seamlessly unfold. I'm not suggesting there won't be some unforeseen situations. However, you can limit the impact these occurrences have on your GFG-Girlfriends' getaway.

Ensure everyone is involved, solicit help and advice, start early, and don't be afraid to discuss all types of situations and circumstances that the group feels are appropriate. This chapter touched on the broader discussion; however, focus on the unique needs of the group. You're almost there and the best laid plans will ensure the GFG—Girlfriends' Getaway will be a trip of a lifetime.

CHAPTER 6

Costs And Finances –
What To Consider

"Can anything be so elegant as to have few wants, and to serve them one's self?"

—*Ralph Waldo Emerson*

"Be a good steward of your finances."

—*Unknown*

CHAPTER 6

COSTS AND FINANCES—
WHAT TO CONSIDER

FINANCIAL CONSIDERATIONS

As we go through our daily lives, finances are an extremely important aspect of living. Financial planning and preparation is important for our basic necessities, educational needs, retirement, personal pleasures, etc. Therefore, planning a GFG—Girlfriends' Getaway can cause hesitation as one reflects on the costs associated with a trip and costs can seem overwhelming. Finances can also cause all sorts of anxieties and the thought of taking a GFG—Girlfriends' Getaway can seem on the surface selfish as one evaluates the financial obligations required from the family budget. According to the 2018 Expedia Vacation Deprivation® study, finances are increasingly a factor for Americans who haven't taken a vacation in the last six months, with 54 percent feeling like they can't afford a trip.

Certainly, one must be mindful of the family income prior to the planning of a GFG—Girlfriends' Getaway in order to maintain a strong sense of financial responsibility. We know in life, financial security is a driving factor in families and relationships. Financial security can enhance a relationship and lack of financial security can complicate a relationship. According to the Divorce magazine and other sources, one of the leading causes of divorce is financial incompatibility. We don't want financial recklessness for married women to be the cause of a "divorce." In the same way, we don't want it to deteriorate your relationships during the GFG—Girlfriends' Getaway. That would be a heavy burden to carry during your trip so you want to ensure you have a well-defined financial plan in place prior to your trip. Even being single requires having a strong financial plan and being mindful of your financial circumstances when embarking on a GFG—Girlfriends' Getaway.

You also don't want "buyer's remorse" during and after your trip. We recognize that a GFG—Girlfriends' Getaway is a financial investment to help secure your peace of mind; however, going into debt is not the responsible way to go about it.

So ask yourself, how do you justify paying for the cost of a moderate to lavish GFG—Girlfriends' Getaway revolving around a single individual in the family? If you step back and take a moment to think about it, most of what we do and many of the financial costs of life are for the benefits of those around us and we sometimes neglect ourselves. We spend on our kids, our spouses, our parents, our friends, and a host of others. We sometimes forget to share the financial love for ourselves. Well, not anymore! Your GFG—Girlfriends' Getaway is that special treat for you and you alone.

Ok, maybe you did buy those nice boots and you also spent extra money on new electronics. Nonetheless, with proper planning, you can find ways to afford paying for an annual or biannual GFG—Girlfriends' Getaway. It may require some moderate sacrifices such as going on a shopping diet and giving up that daily mocha, selling a few pairs of shoes, cutting back on eating out, and saving a little bit from your monthly check. When it's all said and done, you will be surprised that you have now saved enough for your GFG—Girlfriends'

Getaway. You may even have loved ones donate funds for your trip. There are many ways to find the appropriate funds for your GFG—Girlfriends' Getaway. You just have to make it a priority by planning early and being consistent. Now let's connect the investment of a GFG—Girlfriends' Getaway with the "value" of money and happiness over time.

MONEY, VALUE, AND TIME

Many people have numerous perspectives of how they value money and time. Researchers from the University of Pennsylvania and the University of California, Los Angeles (UCLA) looked at the "value" of money by studying 4,400 Americans and the impact of spending on their happiness over time. I believe we should analyze this study as it's very applicable in emphasizing the importance of investing in a GFG—Girlfriends' Getaway and the long-term benefits of that financial investment. Additionally, studies have shown that when people are asked to review their past spending choices, they are least likely to regret vacationing.

The overall results of the study identified four key areas that improved happiness over time as it relates to the spending of money. One might have assumed that spending money on materialistic items demonstrates more "value"; however, according to the study, that's not the case. I was pleased that the GFG—Girlfriends' Getaway "value proposition" of providing women with long-term happiness over time aligns nicely with the UCLA study. The four spending areas below were found to provide the most value in peoples lives:

1. Spending money on extra time (i.e., housekeeping services, etc.)

2. Spending money on great experiences

3. Spending money with someone you care about

4. Spending money on someone else

I wholeheartedly agree with the study results based upon my personal experiences. I may not remember those out-of-season shoes I purchased; however, I will never forget swimming with the dolphins. I may vaguely remember that electronic gadget that ultimately broke or became outdated; however, I will never forget the looks of my girlfriends' faces as the lion walked past our Jeep during an African safari. Those memories bring about a form of happiness that's worth the investment and its long lasting, unlike other materialistic items. A GFG—Girlfriends' Getaway also combines great experiences with people you care about. Make the investment into your overall happiness and it will pay off in multiple dividends over a lifetime.

Let's now discuss establishing a travel budget for your GFG—Girlfriends' Getaway.

TRAVEL BUDGET

Establishing a personal travel budget that corresponds with your travel companions is imperative in order to ensure complete continuity amongst the group. Overpricing a GFG—Girlfriends' Getaway beyond the financial boundaries of each person can be problematic.

FINANCIAL TIPS

- Speak with a financial advisor to assist with evaluating your finances and how to incorporate a GFG—Girlfriends' Getaway along with other travel needs into your financial planning.
- Utilize online tools and apps to monitor and track spending and set goals. There are customized apps that actually manage group travel and financial arrangements.

- Work with your bank to establish a GFG—Girlfriends' Getaway account and/or credit card.

- Delegate one of the travel partners to be the designated treasurer and require monthly payments. This person can also serve as the accountant during the trip.

- For frequent professional travelers, utilize airline, hotel, and car rental perks etc. where applicable to assist in costs.

- Keep track of spending while on your GFG—Girlfriends' Getaway so you can manage spending and you can estimate spending patterns for your next trip. It's nice to have a baseline of spending habits.

Other savings tips include bringing food such as small snacks, protein bars, alcohol and other items you can easily pack to save costs. When traveling internationally, research customs policies regarding food.

If you are determined to do a lavish trip such as a three-week cruise along the Mediterranean, then you have to find travel partners who are financially able to afford such a lavish trip. If your budget is more modest and you want to do a weekend GFG—Girlfriends' Getaway to Las Vegas, then identify those travel partners who are in the same financial situation as you. It's ok for your initial GFG—Girlfriends' Getaway to be modest as you begin to step outside your boundaries. You will ultimately develop the courage and experiences to expand and look to explore more lavish GFG—Girlfriends' Getaways.

Nonetheless, plan accordingly and be mindful. This is where emotional intelligence and sensitivities are important. This is also why you must have these discussions early on. Finances will also dictate critical factors such as location, timing, type of trip, etc., during the planning process. Also, recognize as women, we sometimes spend more than we should, so plan accordingly.

During the planning process, be very clear on the spending rules. Make sure you pay for all of your personal expenditures and stick to it!

For example, when at dinner, either you split the bill equally regardless of what everyone orders, or you get separate checks if possible. If someone pays the entire tab of a meal for convenience, pay them back immediately. It can be very frustrating to have people forget in all the excitement to pay their debts, which can ultimately cause conflict. It is also unfair to the person exhibiting a form of kindness. These are rules that should be clear upfront as to eliminate confusion and hard feelings later.

Also, from a financial standpoint, be mindful of situations that can add undue financial burdens. For example, identify how often the group will go out to restaurants. Find ways to come to a consensus on prices for activities, food, and other cost-sensitive areas.

If possible, find ways to economize your GFG—Girlfriends' Getaway if finances for some are limited. Consider using creativity in finding affordable options during your trip. You will have to delegate who will be responsible for researching and identifying these options, so utilize the skillsets of those in the group as discussed in Chapter 5, "It's in the Details."

During one of my cost-conscious GFG—Girlfriends' Getaways, we rented a vacation home and went to a local grocery store to prepare meals during the trip. It was fun, novel, and financially practical for the group.

When mapping out costs, you may want to consider local options, so find people who know those secret non-tourist spots. Of course, if you're doing an all-inclusive trip, costs are easily manageable. There are many options for inexpensive food, drinks, etc. Don't shy away from trying something new and exotic. Be creative. When exploring food options, you may consider budgeting for an elaborate meal daily and less expensive options throughout the day. Remember, you can design your GFG—Girlfriends' Getaway any way that suits the needs of the group.

I strongly recommend you begin to plan ahead, be consistent, driven, and determined. Do not procrastinate, delay, or simply give up. I've been a part of numerous situations where travel partners weren't financially prepared and had to bail. This can cause tremendous setbacks for the group as you're finalizing rooming, tours, etc. It's also unfair to the group and can get you immediately placed on the "do not invite" lists for future GFG—Girlfriends' Getaways. No one wants to be on that list. Take time to review the financial tips and share during your "Girls' Night Out" discussed in Chapter 4.

SUMMARY OF COSTS AND FINANCES

"Money, like emotions, is something you must control to keep your life on the right track."

—Natasha Munson, *Life Lessons for My Sisters: How to Make Wise Choices and Live a Life You Love!*

In summary, this financial chapter is vitally important in ensuring that you are in a good financial position pre-and post your GFG—Girlfriends' Getaways. You must make the financial commitment early on and involve all those parties necessary to ensure you and your family can afford a GFG—Girlfriends' Getaway. Stay mindful of your financial situation and be considerate of others. Do not put yourself in financial debt because all the benefits of a GFG—Girlfriends' Getaway will diminish from the financial stress. We know for certain that the value of investing in great experiences with close girlfriends will pay off over time. Remain focused and consistent and you will be in a financially good shape for your GFG—Girlfriends' Getaway.

CHAPTER 7

Preparations While Away

"A good plan implemented today is better than a perfect plan implemented tomorrow."

—George Patton

CHAPTER 7

PREPARATIONS WHILE AWAY

*N*ow that your group has secured the location, paid the down payments, and are counting the days before your departure, don't forget to take care of the fundamentals of your household or you could find yourself coming home to a hot mess. Or worse yet, you will get calls, emails, and/or texts that will drive you and your girlfriends crazy and potentially ruin your wonderful GFG—Girlfriends' Getaway. So, what are some of the basics of preparations?

THE BASICS

1. Childcare: If you have children, whether young, early adolescent, or teenager, you will need to make the appropriate preparations to ensure their needs are fully met while you're away. Be sure to have family and friends available to assist your spouse or significant other with the children. Notify your children's schools, if applicable, that you will be out of town potentially during school days. Also have back-up

assistance to ensure that your significant other is not over-whelmed. Remember, if your spouse or significant other is not used to taking full responsibility for the children, you want to ensure they have help. Also, build up their capabili-ties over time to give them the confidence that they can do this while you're away.

Reassure the children that it will be ok to be with their dad or other parent and family members or friends while you're away. My children were accustomed to me leaving due to my extensive professional travel; however, I had travel companions whose families were not used to mom being away for any significant amount of time. Therefore, having a regular "Girls' Nights Out" to plan your GFG—Girlfriends' Getaway will help the children understand that mom is taking time for herself (and will eventually be going away) and they can survive a few hours and ultimately a few days without her. The "Girls' Night Out" is also a nice precursor for your spouse or significant other to get com-fortable with the idea of a GFG—Girlfriends' Getaway. If necessary, bribe the kids with the thoughts of getting cool souvenirs after your trip or use whatever gets them excited and amenable to your GFG—Girlfriends' Getaway. With the advances of electronic devices, you can video chat and leverage technology regularly but don't get overly obsessive. Review Chapter 2, "Convincing Significant Others." They will be fine and if you've made the necessary preparations, things will run smoothly with few glitches.

I've also had mothers ask at what age is it appropriate to leave the kids for a GFG—Girlfriends' Getaway. My response, based upon an infor-mal survey of women travelers with families, is that the age to leave your children varies due to several key factors such as support sys-tems, maturity of the kids, spousal commitment, etc. I've known moth-ers who have taken a short weekend GFG—Girlfriends' Getaway with the support of their spouses when the children were under the age of two. These mothers were overly stressed, and the trip provided them with moments of sanity, time to get some much-needed sleep, and just simply breathe. You must evaluate your home circumstances care-fully, identifying the needs and capabilities of your support base, your own personal mental state, and determine what age makes sense. If your household doesn't have the capability to stand alone, then hold off until you believe they are ready. I would caution that you not use this rationale as a long-term excuse. If your kids are out of diapers and they are in school all day, then you can certainly begin considering a GFG—Girlfriends' Getaway.

2. Food and cleaning: Be sure to stock the house with plenty of food while you're away. Make it easy for your spouse or significant other so that you hear no complaints upon your return. Believe me, it's worth the extra effort. Also, make sure the house is clean and tidy. However, keep in mind, when you return, the house may be a complete wreck. Therefore, if possible, have a cleaning service come prior to your return. Be sure to prepare the cleaning service for the unknown condition of the house.

3. Work preparation: If your GFG—Girlfriends' Getaway occurs during the workdays and you're taking vacation time, be sure to clear all vacationing with your job. Provide sufficient notice to avoid conflicts. This is no different than when you take a vacation with your family; however, it is vitally important that you not allow work to infringe on the time you have dedicated for yourself.

If your communication is going to be limited due to Wi-Fi and location constraints, make sure your job is informed to set expectations. Also, do not carry any work guilt. This time is for you! This GFG—Girlfriends' Getaway is for you to focus on you and only you. Work gets plenty of you and now it's time for you to spoil yourself and find yourself. Therefore, handle your business prior to your trip and leave the work at work.

4. Provide all travel documents and itineraries to family and close friends: Be sure to keep everyone in the loop on where you're going, for how long, etc. It makes everyone feel a lot more at ease with your trip. Make hard copies even though most information can be shared electronically.

5. Begin preparing for what you will wear: For those of us who like to shop, this is a great opportunity to find new items for your trip. Remember, however, to budget because you may want to spend extra money while on your trip. Nonetheless, you will need to begin to prepare for your outfits based on the location, season, activities planned, etc. Be sure to pack appropriately. Overpacking can be costly and clumsy, depending on the vacation location. I have dedicated the next section solely to packing.

6. Other considerations: With so many of life's responsibilities on our shoulders, we must make sure we take care of those additional family needs that may include pets, caregivers' assistance, bills, etc. Resist the urge to stress over every little thing. Remember you are not leaving for a lifetime and most things that you left will be waiting for you upon your return.

PACKING: "A WOMAN'S NIGHTMARE"

Although this is not a typical travel guide, I do want to highlight an area that can be a challenge, specifically for women, and that's packing. I would be remiss not to share both the positives and potential negative pitfalls to proper packing.

For the twenty-plus years I've traveled for work, I have learned how to be extremely refined and particular about what I pack while traveling. Those who know me well would disagree and say that my boots and shoes make it so that I have excessively large and heavy luggage. That might be true; however, I have learned for work travel to pack exactly what I need to wear. I am very lean on my options of attire and very specific. It is extremely rare that I overpack. Let me explain. I define overpacking as having clothes or items that were unused during the trip. To ensure that I don't overpack, I map out my week and assign an outfit for that daily event. I assess the conditions (i.e., a cold meeting room, an outdoor event, casual event, etc.) and pack accordingly. I will say this is a learned skill due to having too many disastrous packing situations.

Ironically, this has not been the case for my personal travel. I have overpacked, underpacked, and just basically screwed up the packing altogether. I have been in situations where having excessive luggage made it difficult to commute in locations that didn't have modern conveniences such as escalators or ramps, and thus, I was lugging heavy pieces of luggage up stairs. A disaster. I've found myself constantly pleading with the airline agent to cut me some slack when my luggage was overweight, and inevitably, I would find myself standing on the side of the counter pulling clothes and items out of my luggage to decrease the weight and not pay exorbitant overweight fees. Try your best to avoid these embarrassing situations. I've known women who have traveled internationally for more than a week with just a carry-on. It can seem shocking but it is possible. I recall reading about a traveler who takes pictures of outfits and stores the pictures in preparation for her trip. This allows her to minimize overpacking. Effective packing is a beautiful skill to acquire.

Underpacking is just as bad. I've had to re-wear clothes when I didn't have access to a washer and dryer. In some circumstances, I didn't even have access to shopping. I've borrowed shoes and clothes from my travel companions during a GFG—Girlfriends' Getaway, which is awkward and simply not cool.

Also keep in mind, while embarking on a GFG—Girlfriends' Getaway (depending on your budget) there's a high probability you're going to purchase things. Whether souvenirs for your family and friends or goodies for yourself, these items are going to have to go somewhere upon returning home. If you haven't allocated space for the newly purchased items, you're going to have to buy additional luggage. Or you're going to have to ask your travel companions to help you out. That's risky because they will have their own goodies.

The packing situation is so important because the airlines have beefed up their restrictions on luggage. Most airlines have restrictions on the number of pieces per passenger and a maximum weight before they assess fees for excessive weight and number of bags. Be sure to know their policies and the costs associated with luggage. The costs may be a deterrent to overpacking. International flights may have weight restrictions even for carry-on luggage, so know the policies.

I would be remiss not to comment on the actual luggage pieces. I would recommend investing in quality and durable pieces of luggage. Ensure that the luggage is sturdy and "lightweight" particularly if you've experienced challenges in the past with heavy luggage. You don't want to add to the weight due to the luggage itself. I have so many different luggage brands, sizes, and styles that I could write a book on luggage alone. I will say that having a wheel fall off of your luggage while you're running through the airport with your girls is certainly comical but no fun if you're the one dragging a broken piece of luggage throughout your trip. Invest wisely.

So, here's some thoughts:

- Know your airline baggage policies! They can be tricky.

- Invest in a solid piece of luggage that is durable and can handle being tossed around and withstand being stuffed.

- Be sure to consider the size and dimensions of your luggage particularly the carry-on luggage. You want to make sure it fits in the overhead bins.

- Map out your daily activities and pack exactly what you need. It's a tough challenge to do if you're not sure how you'll feel that day and you have so many cool outfits to choose from. Also, try to pack shoes that can be worn multiple times. You don't necessarily need a different pair for every outfit. If you need an extra outfit, you can simply buy one while on the trip. Keep it simple. It will make it easier for your travel experience.

- Your toiletries, makeup, hair products, jewelry, and other items should be packed in moderation. I know it may appear to be a difficult feat to accomplish; however, it will make your travel experience so much easier when dashing through airports, which have become increasingly rigid with security measures.

- I would recommend only taking extra undergarments and potentially one spare outfit. You can do this.

- Rolling clothes in the luggage is considered the most efficient form of packing by experts and I would agree.

- Take a spare duffle bag or foldable luggage for additional items you may purchase to eliminate having to purchase luggage while on your trip.

- If you're going to a country that has an abundance of poverty, consider wearing clothes that you are willing to donate to a charitable organization. The recipients of your clothing will be very appreciative of your kindness and generosity.

- Due to my typical heavy luggage and drama at the airport, my girlfriends purchased me a hand scale to weigh my luggage before I embark on a GFG—Girlfriends' Getaway. It was a perfect gift.

SUMMARY OF PREPARATIONS WHILE AWAY

"The smallest step in the right direction, could be the biggest step of your life."

—*Unknown*

In summary, make all the necessary preparations for your GFG—Girlfriends' Getaway, both for at home and the trip, to eliminate interruptions and drama while you're gone. Keep in mind, there may be some glitches but overall you want to prepare your family as best as you can. The preparations benefit both the family and you because it allows you to travel and enjoy the mental and emotional benefits of your GFG—Girlfriends' Getaway, feeling confident that home is well taken care of. But make sure you pack appropriately to maintain a sense of sanity and order.

CHAPTER 8

Disruptor Situations –
No Drama Mama

"Surround yourself with girlfriends that push you to be and do better. No drama or mess. Just higher goals and high heels. Good times and positive energy. No jealousy or shade. Simply bringing out the absolute best in each other."

—Unknown

CHAPTER 8

DISRUPTOR SITUATIONS—
NO DRAMA MAMA

*H*ands down, one of the most important aspects of a GFG—Girlfriends' Getaway that I've heard from women across all ages, professions, personalities, etc. is that they DO NOT WANT ANY DRAMA during a GFG—Girlfriends' Getaway! It's important as women that we play nice while on our GFG—Girlfriends' Getaway. Life brings about enough drama when dealing with work, family, and everyday activities. As a result, when participating in a GFG—Girlfriends' Getaway, it's important that all of your girlfriends set ground rules to ensure that the drama stops once you leave home.

As women, we can come to the table with our own emotional issues; however, drama can be exasperating if your spouse or significant other is contacting you erratically and causing issues, if the kids are acting crazy, or your job insists on infringing on your GFG—Girlfriends' Getaway time. You will have to make it a point to step away and not inflict your drama on your friends. Bringing negativity or drama into the setting can derail the experiences not only for you but for the entire group.

I was part of a situation during a GFG—Girlfriends' Getaway where a travel companion received a souring text from a loved one during the group dinner and instead of shaking it off, she had a bad attitude during the entire evening. It spilled over onto the entire group and spoiled the dinner for everyone. There are countless examples where someone's mood, attitude, or personal disposition can impact an entire GFG—Girlfriends' Getaway. This is why having those hard discussions upfront and knowing your travel companions' personalities and tendencies will determine if you'll find your GFG—Girlfriends' Getaway to be at risk.

If by chance your mood shifts and some personal or professional drama starts to impact your inner self, step aside and deal with it in the most appropriate manner possible. Go to your room, walk along the beach, or simply find a quiet area and breathe. Involving the group can cause an unhealthy vibe. Needless to say, you are with your girlfriends and they may want to provide some modest guidance and support as friends always do, so engage lightly. Again, this is where emotional intelligence and mindfulness of the situation is well applied by both yourself and your travel companions.

CONFLICT AVOIDANCE

During your GFG—Girlfriends' Getaway, you must make an exerted effort to avoid conflict. In our lives conflict is inevitable, so do your best to minimize it from occurring during the GFG—Girlfriends' Getaway. Studies have shown that stress has a tendency to cause drama and conflict during crucial times in our lives. We also know that within any given hour we can experience many different types of emotions. As a result, it can certainly be problematic on a GFG—Girlfriends' Getaway if travel companions are not self-aware. And this doesn't consider other dicey factors such as alcohol. That alter ego in us may manifest itself in full force! So, it's imperative we are fully aware of personal triggers and learn how to manage them amongst women prior to a GFG—Girlfriends' Getaway.

Some notable situations that can cause conflict include the following behaviors during the GFG—Girlfriends' Getaway:

1. Do not allow for traveling partners to try to "gangsta" your trip. The term "gangsta" is a slang term meaning someone behaves as if they are completely in charge over everyone and attempts to control all the situations without everyone's input or agreement. This person can be relentless in bossing everyone around and causing the vibe of the GFG—Girlfriends' Getaway to be stressful and toxic. I am myself a person who can be overly controlling; thus, I know being "gangsta" is something to be mindful of.

This is also where it requires you and your girlfriends to be firm in only participating in activities and events that fit your personal desires. Even if it requires you to do some things alone, that's ok because this trip is for *you*. If you don't stand your ground, you may find your GFG—Girlfriends' Getaway experience to be uninspiring and fruitless.

2. Be sure to stay closely connected to home but not excessively so. If you feel you may get homesick or miss the family too much, then plan a vacation in moderation, i.e., weekend trip vs a week.

3. Try not to be reckless in behaviors that could conflict with the other women. If you choose to binge drink, make sure those with you are fine with it or separate yourself as not to make others feel uncomfortable. Be cautious of reckless behavior that can be detrimental during your GFG—Girlfriends' Getaway.

4. Be in tune with the finances and be very clear on how charges will be accounted for and paid for. If this is not made clear at the beginning of the trip, it can get messy

and cause problems down the road. Review Chapter 6, "Costs and Finances—What to Consider."

5. If someone in the group says something or does something that ticks you off, find a way to address it quickly and let it go. Everyone is working on limited time and to waste time dealing with unhealthy drama is costly both financially and emotionally. During the trip, everyone should do what's necessary to avoid conflict and drama. If an unfortunate situation occurs, agree to resolve it quickly and work to eliminate any negative energy. Realize that some people are more sensitive than others and a crude joke or distasteful comment can cause conflict. Try to avoid those situations.

6. Keep in mind, if you have had experiences with one of your girlfriends who has demonstrated toxic and unhealthy behaviors, I strongly recommend you evaluate whether this travel companion should participate. A GFG—Girlfriends' Getaway is not the venue to hope to change people's personalities or behaviors. So evaluate closely utilizing the compatibility assessments found in Chapter 3, "Who Are Your Girlfriends? Travel Friends."

Don't get me wrong; I'm not recommending you walk on eggshells throughout your GFG—Girlfriends' Getaway. I just want you to be mindful of others and recognize that all of you are on this trip for the fulfillment of lifelong experiences.

MISSING YOUR FAMILY

When you embark on your GFG—Girlfriends' Getaway, there's a high probability that you will miss your family while feeling guilty and contemplating how they would enjoy the experiences you're embarking on. This is normal and not uncommon. My recommendation is to acknowledge these emotions and then begin to remember in a few days you will be back with them and the familiar chaos and real life will be there waiting for you. Also remember that you will have those special travel moments with them during your family vacations and other numerous family gatherings. Relish the moments of your GFG—Girlfriends' Getaway to breathe and find yourself.

Find ways to suppress these emotions as best you can. You don't want them to place a damper on your GFG—Girlfriends' Getaways and you definitely don't want to cause a rippling effect with your travel companions. During various GFG—Girlfriends' Getaways, we've had to rein in girlfriends who became overly obsessed with missing their family. We simply reminded them of the many reasons for embarking on a GFG—Girlfriends' Getaway and pulled them back into the moment. Works every time.

SUMMARY OF DISRUPTOR SITUATIONS AND NO DRAMA

"As your life changes so will your circle."

—Unknown

In summary, you are embarking on a GFG—Girlfriends' Getaway to get away from the stresses of life and to find calming moments to breathe, live, learn, and laugh. Negative drama and disruptive situations can derail all your efforts and that of your girlfriends. It is imperative to do whatever is necessary to avoid these situations. I've heard of women fighting during vacationing, women cutting their trip short and leaving, friendships ending, and other unfortunate outcomes due to lack of emotional intelligence, empathy, and restraint. Work hard to identify the right travel companions and upfront develop mitigation strategies. It's an unfortunate topic but necessary as we all know life happens.

CHAPTER 9

The Vacation

"Beast Mode."

"And the adventure begins."

CHAPTER 9

THE VACATION

GOING IT ALONE

Here's a novel idea for those who may be struggling to find girlfriends who aren't available due to life's circumstances: "GO IT ALONE." It's certainly a different experience than traveling with your girls but it can bring its own rewards. It will take serious contemplation and evaluation; however, you can walk away feeling equally as rejuvenated as with a group of women. You will have to be a person who's highly confident and secure within yourself. If you don't mind eating in a restaurant alone, going to a concert alone, or taking simple walks along the beach alone, then "going it alone" is certainly an option. As a business traveler, I often travel alone and enjoy the solitude of being able to please my own personal desires without making compromises. Going it alone will provide you with the opportunity to make new friends, enjoy your own thoughts, and find the time to recreate yourself in the midst of your own personal journey. It's definitely worth exploring for you road warriors. I've had a few friends travel alone on cruises, trips to the Middle East, and even a simple weekend trip to New York City. It's doable and possible. Remember, it's all about you!

For married women or those in a committed relationship, this may be a heavier lift of a discussion to have with a significant other. They may find it difficult to understand the need for you to want to go off and vacation alone without them or girlfriends. It can be hard for people to grasp this unique personal need and it will take a heartfelt discussion and a very understanding person to give you the wings to fly and live your life. This special person also can't harbor insecurities; otherwise, it will be a nonstarter. Nevertheless, it's worth exploring and may take you to another level of self-awareness. Just another option to consider for the modern woman.

HEALTH AND WELLNESS

"Sore today, strong tomorrow."

—Unknown

As a part of your trip and planning, it's important to make sure everyone is aware of the physical compatibilities of your travel companions (review Chapter 3, "Compatibility—Travel Friends"). Health and wellness is extremely important in your daily lives and equally important during a GFG—Girlfriends' Getaway. Ensure that during the capability assessment, health status is taken into account. This can have a significant impact on the type of trip and location. Everyone has varying degrees of stamina and endurance. Make sure they align appropriately to avoid confusion and unfortunate health consequences.

That means consider your health, both physically and emotionally. Being healthy is a life requirement that makes you a better person and allows for you to gain the greatest fulfillment of your trip. It is important that you have a healthy mind and body so that you can do a variety of activities that a GFG—Girlfriends' Getaway can provide.

While on a cruise during a GFG—Girlfriends' Getaway, my back, surprisingly to me, went out. I had never experienced such an injury before and was shocked because I believed I was in pretty good shape. However, over the course of the year prior to the GFG—Girlfriends' Getaway, I had put on a significant amount of weight and was slacking in my regimen of a healthy lifestyle. As a result of my injury, I met with the ship's physician who prescribed medication and she also recommended that I stay in my room for the duration of the cruise to recover. I thought she was nuts and against her advice ventured off to an island with my girlfriends. During the excursion, I thought I was going to die because I had significant difficulty walking and the drugs were making me extremely sleepy. My situation also made it difficult for my travel companions who unfortunately had to accommodate me during my pain. Fortunately, once I made it back to my room and got some rest, I was able to finish out the cruise with nominal pain. However, it could have been worse. It could have truly ruined the GFG—Girlfriends' Getaway experience for me and negatively impacted my travel companions.

In addition, make sure you come prepared with all your medications and health supplies and know your limitations. For example, if you get seasick, be sure to have motion sickness medication or decline activities that require excessive motion such as boating activities, etc. I've been on a few GFG—Girlfriends' Getaways where someone experiences seasickness and it was not fun for them or the group. So be cognizant of your health limitations prior to your GFG—Girlfriends' Getaway. Also, be sure to take your insurance card and know how to access healthcare both domestically and internationally.

Your Mind: Your mind must also be healthy when going on a GFG—Girlfriends' Getaway. We know that the purpose of a GFG—Girlfriends' Getaway is to strengthen your heart, mind, and soul; however, there needs to be a baseline of serenity. Otherwise, it be could be a disaster for you and your girlfriends. It's understandable that you may have much drama at home and work prior to the trip; however, if you're going through mental challenges such as depression, severe anxieties, or a host of other medical illnesses, it may make sense to get those issues under control prior to participating in a GFG—Girlfriends' Getaway.

Sleep: Sleep is considered one of the three pillars of health along with exercise and a healthy diet. The benefits of sleep for the heart, weight, and mind are immense. So during your GFG—Girlfriends' Getaway, find some time to get rest. Sometimes this can be difficult because there are so many exciting and new activities that the group may want to experience; however, take the time to sleep and reap the benefits. It's an important part of strengthening your spirit.

Massages, body scrubs, etc.: It is imperative I recommend that during your GFG—Girlfriends' Getaway, you find time to do some relaxing soft activities that may include full body massages, body scrubs, facials, yoga, or other outings that can allow you to fully breathe and exhale. These are the type of special moments that can be done with your girls and heighten the experiences by providing long-term benefits.

SAFETY

As mature women, we recognize the importance of being mindful of safety measures and our surroundings while traveling. During your planning, you should assess all safety considerations on locations, hotels, etc. Using common sense measures will eliminate dangerous situations. Addressing safety concerns upfront will also benefit concerns of loved ones.

During the planning, delegate someone to do research and assess the safety considerations for your destination (review Chapter 5, "It's in the Details"). Have a plan in place to mitigate risks.

SOCIAL MEDIA: "FRIEND OR FOE?"

Years ago when I started participating in a GFG—Girlfriends' Getaway, social media was a small part of the adventure. Mobile devices were limited, costly to use, and did not have the capabilities they have today. Social media was basically nonexistent. Today, social media is vast across numerous platforms and has changed how our lives are portrayed and showcased to a broader group of family and friends. As a result, when with your girlfriends, be sure to define the social media etiquette and guidelines prior to the journey. This will eliminate those embarrassing situations where you find your exposed hips showcased on various media platforms.

Guidelines to consider:

1. Pictures should be posted after approval by those in the pictures.

2. Comments about the GFG—Girlfriends' Getaway on social media should be discussed.

3. The use of technology during dinners and social gatherings should be discussed. It's important to be in the moment, so be mindful of technology use during outings.

4. When asking people to take pictures of you, do so in moderation. Remember this is also their vacation and not your exclusive photoshoot.

5. Be cautious about letting your social media desires dictate your daily adventures as this can potentially put the security of your home at risk. Be aware and use good judgement of how you make yourself and the group exposed during the GFG—Girlfriends' Getaway.

MOBILE DEVICE ETIQUETTE: RULES OF ENGAGEMENT

This is a topic that is extremely vital in ensuring you and your girlfriends are living in the moment and are not constantly texting while in a group setting and being distracted by things occurring outside of the travel moments. It is worth a conversation during your "Girls' Night Out" discussed in Chapter 4 to gauge the importance of placing limitations on mobile device distractions. Come into agreement on mobile device rules of engagement. These can include limiting mobile device use during dinners, establishing a phone-free time, keeping the mobile devices out of sight during certain events, etc. It is important to be considerate and respectful. In some situations, excessive mobile device use can demonstrate lack of awareness and sensitivity to the group as a whole. Determine what works best for the group and adhere to it.

As a caveat to mobile device rules of engagement, the makeup of the group will significantly define those rules. It may be completely acceptable by the group to have unlimited mobile device freedom so just ensure the discussion occurs on the front end to eliminate awkward moments.

JOURNALING AND RECORDING OF EVENTS

One of the many lessons I've learned while traveling is making the effort to record the adventures, whether through electronics or writing down events in a journal. There are many reasons for this. First and foremost, there is no way you will remember every little detail of your adventure, so document situations that occur at the start of the trip, i.e., funny hiccups, beautiful landscapes, tour adventures, and other memorable events that make you laugh and are memories that will last a lifetime. My girlfriends and I often grab our journals and relive many wonderful moments. It will lighten the heart and remind you of how wonderful life can be. You can even share the "clean" versions with your family and they will also find enjoyment in the world of travel.

Although I believe in recording exciting travel moments, I also believe in living in the moment. So, I may do a short clip and then sit back and enjoy. As my mother always says, "Life is for the living."

SUMMARY OF THE VACATION

"Done! You did it!"

Whether going it alone or with your girlfriends, your GFG—Girlfriends' Getaway will be filled with opportunities to maintain good health and wellness. You will also enjoy sharing with friends and family your adventures via social media during and after your GFG—Girlfriends' Getaway while capturing many lifetime events. Cherish these pleasures and maintain a sense of courtesy for your travel companions.

CHAPTER 10

Returning Home: Vacation Mode — The Game Changer

"Every morning that you wake up is another chance to get it right."

—*Unknown*

CHAPTER 10

RETURNING HOME: VACATION MODE– THE GAME CHANGER

*U*pon returning home from your GFG—Girlfriends' Getaway, you should be in a euphoric mood. Your positive mental state should transcend both in your personal and professional lives. My family and friends always appreciate how at peace I am upon returning from a GFG—Girlfriends' Getaway and how much more tolerable I am of many situations. All the benefits of your trip that we discussed in previous chapters will cultivate themselves upon your return.

Recent studies have shown that parents with strong mental health are likely to raise successful children as they provide effective guidance, love, and most importantly, lead by example. A successful GFG—Girlfriends' Getaway will help you with your mental and emotional stability, thus providing a wealth of benefits to your family.

Your spouse or significant other will also enjoy the smiles and laughter that you will share about your experiences. They will also appreciate how a GFG—Girlfriends' Getaway will enhance those wonderful qualities that they have grown to love and appreciate in you.

When you return to work from a GFG—Girlfriends' Getaway, you will continue your vacation mode that will help you excel at your job. Your boss will wonder what has come over you. That's because you took the time for a "respite." A time to find yourself!

The 2018 Expedia Vacation Deprivation® study also showcases how vacations strengthen relationships. The study showed that 90 percent of people agree that vacations help them feel better connected to their friends and family, 82 percent of people come back from vacation with more patience for their colleagues and clients and lastly, 80 percent agree vacations strengthen their relationship with their significant other.

As discussed in the Introduction, in order to change outcomes, it starts with experiences. As a result, experiences begin to change beliefs and beliefs change actions, ultimately leading to positive outcomes. A GFG—Girlfriends' Getaway will change how you interface with those closest to you. It will broaden your mind because the experiences will foster the beliefs that drive your actions. You will enhance your learnings and a GFG—Girlfriends' Getaway will make you better in the many things you attempt to accomplish.

In my experiences, I've seen women become transformed and are now better because of a GFG—Girlfriends' Getaway. They see the world through a different lens and this makes life better for their family, friends, employer, and community.

Vacation mode will linger, and you will be excited at the thought of planning the next GFG—Girlfriends' Getaway for the next year and beyond. It's addictive and the rewards and benefits are immeasurable.

I would recommend immediately capturing and documenting your experiences so it's fresh. Have a recap "Girls' Night Out" to pull together pictures and memories. It's an opportunity to extend the

GFG—Girlfriends' Getaway and maintain the bonding. This is your time so celebrate and remember the joys of a lifetime.

GAME CHANGER

In your life there are many events that are "Game Changers." Aside from getting married, having kids, buying a car or home, a career change, loss of family, or other extraordinary events, I assure you that investing in a GFG—Girlfriends' Getaway will be an event to add to the list of game changers. It will be considered a game-changing event because it will empower you in many ways, impacting countless aspects of your life. Whether it's becoming more aware of the world and others sharing it with you, fostering friendships, or simply gaining a better understanding of who you are and your purpose, it will all be worth it.

If you plan appropriately and have a wonderful experience, it will be a successful accomplishment—a game changer. You will look for ways to embark on a GFG—Girlfriends' Getaway and elevate your game year after year.

CHAPTER 11

Summary And Conclusion

"She believed she could, so she did."

—Unknown

"Not to spoil the ending for you, but everything is going to be great!"

—Unknown

"Love deeply, eat well, travel often, laugh always."

—Unknown

"Because you are alive, everything is possible."

—Thich Nhat Hanh

CHAPTER 11
SUMMARY AND CONCLUSION

I was recently sitting in a Midwestern restaurant bar waiting to have dinner with friends, and I starting talking with a mature couple about travel. They were a lovely couple both in retirement, albeit struggling with a number of physical ailments. They expressed how they had limited travel experiences due to family, finances and work obligations. In my mind, I noted how these were common excuses for not embarking on those dreams of travel.

As we engaged extensively about travel, they shared with me their dreams of traveling to places such as Australia, New York City, and countless other locations. Their eyes beamed with excitement at the thought of running along the shores of Barcelona. And with each thought and desire there was also an excuse why they couldn't go or why now was not the right time. They blamed their adult kids requiring more of their time, their pets, fear of long plane rides, and the list just kept going. As I listened intently, I was so grateful that the spirit of travel touched my soul early in life and while I'm still physically, mentally, and emotionally capable of enjoying the moments that take you to levels of life that only other avid travelers can understand.

As I continued to engage with the couple, I gently provided them with a vivid picture of Sydney, Australia and simply encouraged that they stop making excuses. I impelled them to take the leap of travel before they lose the opportunity and ultimately live with regrets. They kindly thanked me, and we parted ways. I'm writing this book so that you don't find yourself in the situation where you're looking back with regrets.

A GFG—Girlfriends' Getaway unites all women regardless of differences in age, race, ethnicity, or income. The benefits know no boundaries.

Life is short and moments in time come and go, but some moments will last a lifetime in your memory. The time you spend getting to find yourself are experiences that will carry you throughout the year when faced with many challenges. The GFG—Girlfriends' Getaway will sustain you and help carry you through the good and bad. It will make you a better person to all those who know you and need you. Trust me, you will be wiser and not to mention cool.

Aside from family engagements, my fondest memories are not the designer bag purchases, the fancy shoes, clothes, jewelry and other non-sustaining materialistic things, but those unforgettable precious moments of travel with those whom I share a common bond. Studies have proven it and I can truly testify on behalf of this fact. As I calmly drink coffee from one of my Starbuck's cup collection from all over the world or touch my Pandora bracelet with beads from countless countries, I'm constantly reminded of living my best life.

Do not delay. Stop making excuses and do not put off what you know you can do today. Remember, tomorrow is never promised. These trips are part of the journey of life, a new life, an enhanced life of a woman. And at the end of the day, your family and friends will encourage you to explore these new opportunities once they see the benefits derived from releasing your soul. Bon Voyage!

—*Vikki D*

CHAPTER 12

Personal Quotes From Empowered
Women Who Embrace
GFG-Girlfriends' Getaway

CHAPTER 12
PERSONAL QUOTES FROM EMPOWERED WOMEN WHO EMBRACE GFG-GIRLFRIENDS' GETAWAY'S

*T*he following experiences highlight personal and sincere reflections from a diverse group of women and their viewpoints on traveling with their girls. I felt compelled to have the final thoughts about a GFG—Girlfriends' Getaway end with their wonderful words.

Aged 20-30+:

Rachel: "When I go to a new place, it gives me the opportunity to be myself freely and unapologetically, while learning about a culture unlike my own. Traveling with my friends and family is not only fun but it grants us the chance to build unforgettable moments together. It empowers me to enjoy the beauty and treasures of this world. People tend to ask me why I travel so much, and I always say, 'You only get one life so do yourself a favor and live it up!' Life is limitless."

Melanie: "Traveling with your girlfriends is undeniably a great experience that adds a different level of fun to the trip overall. It's where memories are created, countless pictures are taken, and many laughable moments are made.

It's a time for bonding, relaxing, and basking in the ambiance of the trip itself, but more importantly I believe it adds more to a friendship and sisterhood. It's one thing to travel by yourself or with family, but it's a complete different experience when you can do it with your girlfriends. These are the memories that you'll remember forever and look back on them and laugh and smile.

I've traveled with my best friend countless number of times and visited multiple countries and each time is different but always extremely fun. It's amazing to be exposed and cross countries off the list while visiting major places and experiencing the journey together. I've been to places I never thought I would go, and she has also been there to help me face some fears or push me to do things I never thought I would do which has impacted me overall and made our bond even stronger!

This is an example of the beauty of traveling with your girlfriends. It's an experience like no other!"

Morgan: "Traveling to a destination is like a thrilling new adventure. Every trip is a chapter in a book to reflect on year after year. But the most exciting part of it all is to be able to experience these moments together with your best girlfriends."

Aged 40-50+

Marilyn: "There's an old saying, 'It's better to see something once than hear about it a thousand times.' When I was a little girl, I would read about traveling to many places. It gave me the ability to live outside of where I lived. Today I've had the ability to visit many different places and I feel very blessed that I had the opportunity to see those things for myself with other women who share the same passion."

Elise: "I've been many places and seen many faces and learned many things... all made better because I was in the company of my friends The sunset over the pyramids in Giza, rains on the Christ Redeemer statute in Brazil, the smells of Burj Khalifa in Dubai, fog on table mountain in Cape Town, sitting at the base of the Eiffel Tower in Paris, enjoying the gardens of Alhambra palace in Granada (Spain)... breathtaking and peaceful, it took so much to get there and so much to admire. I came from a single mother, living in the projects and told I'd never amount to anything... I learned to appreciate the blessings, share the laughs and teach my son how to love the world we live in."

Pep: "Traveling with girlfriends is food for the soul because of the special connection you have with them that allows you to truly be yourself and totally relax. A rejuvenating experience and a must for complete wellness!"

Aged 70+

Maxine: "My experiences of a lifetime of travel has revolutionized my life and opened my eyes on how I view the world and people. I've been fortunate enough to share these experiences with women closest to me. Even at my age and with the societal uncertainties, I plan on continuing my journeys of travel because it's such an intricate part of who I am. I would encourage everyone to make traveling with your closest friends an important part of your life."

Sources

SOURCES

CHAPTER 1

"Vacation." *Merriam-Webster,* n.d. Web. 26 June 2017. https://www.merriam-webster.com/dictionary/vacation.

Joseph B. Bayer, Matthew Brook O'Donnell, Christopher N. Cascio & Emily B. Falk., "Brain Sensitivity to Exclusion is Associated with Core Network Closure." *Nature.com,* (2018). Scientific Reports volume 8, Article number: 16037. https://www.nature.com/articles/s41598-018-33624-3.

Nawijn, J., Marchand, M.A., Veenhoven, R. et al. "Vacationers Happier, but most not Happier After a Holiday." *Applied Research Quality Life,* (2010). 5: 35. https://doi.org/10.1007/s11482-009-9091-9.

"Half of Americans aren't taking a summer vacation," *Bankrate.com,* Web. 12 May 2018.
https://www.bankrate.com/personal-finance/smart-money/survey-cant-afford-summer-vacation/.

"Vacation Deprivation® Study." *Expedia,* 16 October 2018. https://newsroom.expedia.com/2018-10-16-American-vacation-deprivation-levels-at-a-five-year-high.

De Bloom, J., Geurts, S.A.E. & Kompier, M.A.J. J. "Vacation (After-) Effects on Employee Health and Well-being, and the Role of Vacation Activities, Experiences and Sleep." *Journal of Happiness Studies*, (2013). 14: 613. https://doi.org/10.1007/s10902-012-9345-3.

Nawijn, J., Marchand, M.A., Veenhoven, R. et al. "Vacationers Happier, but most not Happier After a Holiday." *Applied Research Quality Life, (2010)*. 5: 35. https://doi.org/10.1007/s11482-009-9091-9.

Framington Heart Study research at www.framinghamheartstudy.org.

Vatsal Chikani, MPH, BHMS; Douglas Reding, MD, MPH; Paul Gunderson, PhD; Catherine A. McCarty, PhD, MPH. "Vacations Improve Mental Health Among Rural Women: The Wisconsin Rural Women's Health Study." *Wisconsin Medical Journal, (2005)*. Volume 104, No. 6. https://www.wisconsinmedicalsociety.org/_WMS/publications/wmj/pdf/104/6/20.pdf.

"Vacation Deprivation® Study." *Expedia*, 16 October 2018. https://newsroom.expedia.com/2018-10-16-American-vacation-deprivation-levels-at-a-five-year-high.

Center for Educational Excellence. "Work and Well-Being Survey." *American Psychological Association,* June 2018. http://www.apaexcellence.org/assets/general/2018-work-and-wellbeing-survey-results.pdf?

Carter, C.S. "Neuroendocrine Perspectives on Social Attachment and Love." *Psychoneuroendocrinology*, (1998). 23, 779-818.

Ackerman, Diane. "A Natural History of Love." *Vintage Books*, (1994). ISBN 0-679-76183-7.

Healy, Melissa. "Science Confirms that Women Reap Health Benefits from Friendships." LA Times, 15 June 2005. https://www.seattletimes.com/seattle-news/health/science-confirms-that-women-reap-health-benefits-from-friendships.

Seattle Times, 15 June 2005. https://www.seattletimes.com/seattle-news/health/science- confirms- that-women-reap-health-benefits-from-friendships/.

Weber, Michael. "What is the Link between Love and Oxytocin." *Medical News Today*, 4 September 2017. https://www.medicalnewstoday.com/articles/275795.php.

Stephanie Pappas. "Oxytocin: Facts About the Cuddle Hormone", *Life=Science*, 4 June 2015. https://www.livescience.com/42198-what-is-oxytocin.html.

Pillai, Jagan A and Joe Verghese. "Social Networks and Their Role in Preventing Dementia." *Indian Journal of Psychiatry,* (2009). vol. 51 Suppl 1,5: S22-8.

Center for Educational Excellence. "Work and Well-Being Survey", *American Psychological Association,* June 2018. http://www.apaexcellence.org/assets/general/2018-work-and-wellbeing-survey-results.pdf?

Healy, Melissa. "Science Confirms that Women Reap Health Benefits from Friendships." *LA Times*, 15 June 2005. https://www.seattletimes.com/seattle-news/health/science-confirms-that-women-reap-health-benefits-from-friendships.

"Oxytocin." *Merriam-Webster*, n.d. Web. 18 January 2018. https://www.merriam-webster.com/dictionary/oxytocin.

"Oxytocin Basics." *Psychology Today*, January 2019. https://www.psychologytoday.com/us/basics/oxytocin.

"Sisterhood." *Dictionary.com*, Web. 12 September 2016. https://www.dictionary.com/browse/sisterhood.

R. I. M. Dunbar, Rebecca Baron, Anna Frangou, Eiluned Pearce, Edwin J. C. van Leeuwen, Julie Stow, Giselle Partridge, Ian MacDonald, Vincent Barra, and Mark van Vugt. "Social Laughter is Correlated with an Elevated Pain Threshold." *Proceedings of the Royal Society B: Biological Sciences,* (2011).279. http://doi.org/10.1098/rspb.2011.1373.

Joseph B. Bayer, Matthew Brook O'Donnell, Christopher N. Cascio & Emily B. Falk. "Brain Sensitivity to Exclusion is Associated with Core Network Closure." *Nature.com,* (2018). Scientific Reports volume 8, Article number: 16037. https://www.nature.com/articles/s41598-018-33624-3.

CHAPTER 3
"Apprehension." *Dictionary.com*, Web. 18 February 2018. https://www.dictionary.com/browse/apprehension.

"Compatibility." *Merriam-Webster*, n.d. Web. 2 March 2016. https://www.merriam-webster.com/dictionary/compatibility.

Wikipedia contributors. "Big Five Personality Traits." *Wikipedia, The Free Encyclopedia*, Web. 13 January 2019. https://en.wikipedia.org/wiki/Big_Five_personality_traits.

CHAPTER 4
Clarke, Patrick. "The Benefits of Taking Your Time to Plan a Vacation." *Travel Pulse*, 24 January 2017. https://www.travelpulse.com/news/features/the-benefits-of-taking-your-time-to-plan-a-vacation.html.

CHAPTER 6
"Vacation Deprivation® Study." *Expedia*, 16 October 2018. https://newsroom.expedia.com/2018-10-16-American-vacation-deprivation-levels-at-a-five-year-high.

Summers, Leticia. "5 Surprisingly Common Causes of Divorce." *Divorce*, 17 August 2018. http://www.divorcemag.com/articles/surprisingly-common-causes-of-divorce.

Hershfield, Hal E., et al. "People Who Choose Time Over Money Are Happier." *Social Psychological and Personality Science*, (2016). vol. 7, no. 7. pp. 697–706. doi:10.1177/1948550616649239.

CHAPTER 8

Preston, Cathy. "A Week or Longer Spent in Close rPoximity
with Family or Friends can Sometimes Lead to Vacation Drama."
HUFFPOST, 13 June 2016.
https://www.huffingtonpost.ca/cathy-preston/
vacation-group-travel-drama_a_23450733.

CHAPTER 9

Daskal, Lolly. "Sleep: 4 Scientific Reasons Vacations Are Good for
Your Health." *Inc.com*, 13 June 2016. https://www.inc.com/lolly-das-
kal/4-scientific-reasons-why-vacation-is-awesome-for-you.html.

Center for Organizational Excellence. "Work and Well-Being
Survey", *American Psychological Association*, June 2018. http://
www.apaexcellence.org/assets/general/2018-work-and-wellbe-
ing-survey-results.pdf?

CHAPTER 10

"Vacation Deprivation® Study." *Expedia*. 16 October 2018. https://
newsroom.expedia.com/2018-10-16-American-vacation-deprivation-
levels-at-a-five-year-high.

Photo locations: United States, France, Brazil,
Cuba, Greece, China, Mexico, Australia
